VIKING

At the Water's Edge

A Fisherman's Progress around Britain

Text & illustrations by
BENJAMIN PERKINS

VIKING

VIKING

Published by the Penguin Group
27 Wrights Lane, London W8 5TZ, England
Viking Penguin Inc., 40 West 23rd Street, New York, New York 10010, USA
Penguin Books Australia Ltd, Ringwood, Victoria, Australia
Penguin Books Canada Ltd, 2801 John Street, Markham, Ontario, Canada L3R 1B4
Penguin Books (NZ) Ltd, 182–190 Wairau Road, Auckland 10, New Zealand

Penguin Books Ltd, Registered Offices: Harmondsworth, Middlesex, England

First published 1989
10 9 8 7 6 5 4 3 2 1

Produced and designed by
SAVITRI BOOKS LTD
Southbank House
Suite 106, Black Prince Road
London SE1 7SJ

Art direction by Mrinalini Srivastava
Edited by Wendy Lee

Typeset in Palatino by Dorchester Typesetting Group Ltd, Dorchester, Dorset
Reproduction by Dot Gradations Ltd, Chelmsford, Essex
Printed and bound in Italy by Motta, Milan

A CIP catalogue record for this book is available from the British Library

ISBN 0-670-82597-2

Frontispiece. *The Iorsa Water in spate, with a cock wheatear surveying the scene.*

Below. *Common blue butterfly.*

Contents

A Prejudiced View

The small village where I live is enclosed by a wide bend of the River Stour which, for much of its length, marks the boundary between the counties of Essex and Suffolk. Chance brought me to this area in the first place, and habit and familiarity keep me here, but for a passionate game-fisher and lover of wild places it is not, perhaps, an ideal location; for the Stour, like most of the rivers in this corner of Britain, is quintessentially a coarse-fishing river and all too often, today, the land is drained and cultivated right to the river bank.

I am, therefore, a holiday fisherman pure and simple, and as such have not the smallest claim to any kind of expertise. In this book I offer neither instruction nor advice, my only aim being to impart, if possible, some of the intense delight that I have had, over the years, from fishing beautiful and often remote waters, up and down the British Isles.

As a boy I did a lot of coarse fishing, and a delightful, gentle and contemplative sport it is, but there is a natural tendency in life gradually to progress from one favourite pastime to another, and today I fish only for game fish. I seldom use anything but fly, which statement will be, to some fishermen, as a red rag to a bull. 'Oh,' I hear them cry, disgust in their voices, 'so you are a *purist*!' I suppose I am, to some extent, but I have no objections to the methods used by other fishermen, so long as they are sporting and reasonable in the circumstances, and I acknowledge that some of them – such as

The River Stour at Liston, on the borders of Suffolk and Essex: a quintessential coarse-fishing river.

worming for salmon – require considerable skill. I fly-fish because that is what I enjoy doing. These days I don't worm or spin or troll, because catching fish by those methods gives me less satisfaction. There is no self-imposed rule involved, only choice. If, at any future time, I should fancy trying some method other than fly to catch a fish, I shall use it without any pangs of secret guilt, as I have done in the past. Having said all that, I must admit that there are some waters which are so perfectly suited to fly-fishing that I do feel a twinge of anguish when I see them defaced by the soulless spinner, and I think that there is a strong case for applying the fly-only rule more widely on certain waters and in certain conditions.

Perhaps there is a fundamental difference in attitude between those anglers who are driven to anger by the thought of anyone not making use of every available method of catching fish, and such as me. I fish to catch fish, and feel as much excitement as anyone, I believe, when I am successful, but it is the whole experience, not just the capture, that makes fishing, for me, such a fascinating pastime. The long climb, by stalkers' track, to a high lochan; waiting, at the reedy fringe of a chalk stream, for the rise to start; prospecting the likely lies in a salmon pool; witnessing the awesome spectacle of a river in spate, or rowing home in the twilight across the placid waters of a loch; all these activities, and many more, are as integral a part of the enjoyment of fishing as the hooking or landing of a fish. I am not highly endowed with what Charles St John called 'the organ of destructiveness', nor am I, as Moray McLaren claimed to be, 'a greedy fisherman'. He used the phrase in the sense of never being satisfied, however many fish he had caught, but always wanting one fish more until the day's end. Given such powerful motivation I might be a more successful fisherman. As it is I feel a slight distaste when I read about huge baskets of fish being taken. To my mind, it is the business of netsmen and fish-farms to provide fish for the market. The sporting fisherman should surely be content to kill only what fish he needs for his own and his friends' use, and to release the surplus. I think that I would derive vastly more pleasure from catching three or four really good fish, which I had to work for, than in catching a great multitude, though I readily admit that the matter has never yet been put truly to the test. On the rare occasions when I have encountered fish in a distinctly suicidal mood, they have always come to their senses and gone off the take, long before there was any danger of my being sickened by hecatombs of dead fish on the bank. I have stayed my hand and allowed a hen salmon, heavy with spawn, to swim away, rather than reach for the priest. Admittedly I have only done so once, but then my total tally of salmon is very small by the standards of those with greater skills and much more time to devote to fishing. I felt rather good about it – a self-righteous glow, you may say. After all, the enjoyable part of fish-catching lies in attracting, hooking and playing the fish to the net or the bank, rather than in whacking the poor creature on its head. However, there is another element of enjoyment: that of displaying your catch when you get home to any who will consent to look and to marvel. The trouble lies in the fact that all too often there is no witness to the generous act, and that makes it harder to perform. Nothing is more irritating than the look of veiled disbelief which comes into people's eyes when you tell them you could have had more fish, but that you let the rest go – it rivals even the reaction which generally greets the descriptions of 'the big one that got away'!

One attribute that I may claim, and which perhaps absolves me from being absolutely a poor fisherman, is that I can fish quite happily for long periods without becoming bored or overly dispirited by lack of success. The least successful fisherman, in my experience, is the one who quickly loses heart. He starts off full of enthusiasm, but soon becomes restless; he moves from one place to another, frequently changes his fly, goes off to see how the rod downstream is faring, sits disconsolately on the bank and at the end of the day wonders why he has caught no fish. The really dedicated angler, on the other hand, fishes with concentration all day long, and never misses a chance. I come somewhere in between: so long as conditions are reasonably propitious I keep on fishing, but if everything goes very quiet, my attention does tend to wander. I may miss the odd fish as a result, but the distractions – the deer on the hill, the bird in the air, flowers on the bank, insects dancing over the water – constitute, for me, a vital element in the enjoyment of a day's fishing. These, and the views of sky and landscape glimpsed between tree trunks or over rocks or reed beds as you move along the stream, and most of all the ever-changing nature of the water as it progresses from brawling rapid to smooth glide and from streamy run to deep, still pool, are the very essence of the sport. To read the water, to guess at the topography hidden or obscured by the reflections on its surface and the resulting slacks and currents which determine where the fish are lying, is half the art of fishing.

I do not much enjoy fishing popular reservoirs or other 'put and take' waters. I prefer, if possible, to fish for wild fish in wild places, either on my own or with a congenial companion. The biggest trout I have ever caught was from a well-known reservoir, and I have all but forgotten the details of the encounter, whereas I vividly recall the capture of many a smaller fish where the surroundings, and all the incidents that made up the day's sport, combined to make the occasion memorable. This is not to say that I scorn the pursuit of big fish – far from it: all the time that I am fishing I fantasize about the 'whopper' that may be lurking, unseen, beneath the

July riverside: a pair of tufted duck fly upstream.

ripples. And although I have never, in my life, caught anything that could be described by that epithet (a 6¼-pound tench perhaps came nearest to qualifying), I am well aware of the thrill of catching any fish that is 'big' in relative terms – a pounder, for instance, from a water where the average size of the fish was three to the pound. Many years ago I was fishing

9

the Blairquhan water of the River Girvan in Ayrshire, where the trout, if my memory serves me correctly, averaged about ½ pound or less, and I remember watching a friend hook and land, one evening, a lovely yellow trout of 2 pounds 6 ounces. It was most exciting. The knowledge that in any water there is liable to be the odd fish or two that has managed to beat the average and outgrow all his brethren, adds a peculiar zest to the sport.

There is much to be said for getting to know one particular water really well, and some among my angling acquaintances return year after year to some favoured stretch of water, building up, over a long period, an intimate knowledge of all its moods. They get to know where the best fish lie, according to the height of the water, what lures to use and how to fish, effectively, the tricky places. They know which pieces of water seldom or never yield fish, and can pass them by, and they know where it pays to fish slowly and thoroughly, covering every inch of the water. In theory they should catch more fish than the stranger who has to rely on guesswork and intuition, though it must be said this is not invariably the case. For me, the advantages of having this sort of close relationship with a river are outweighed by the pleasures of discovering, exploring and fishing a water that is entirely unfamiliar. But I do like, also, to return at intervals to favourite places where I can profit from past experience.

No two rivers or lakes are quite alike. The scenery, for one thing, is always unique, and although the associated natural history may be very similar on rivers of the same type and in the same locality, it is never identical: there are always small differences in soil and habitat that can result in an unexpected sighting. And the fishing itself is always different, presenting new challenges wherever one goes. No fisherman can assume that the trout in one water will take the same lure, presented

Ben Stack across Loch More from Aultanrynie. In the evening the hinds come down to graze at the loch edge.

in the same manner, as those in the last water that he fished. Their feeding habits vary from one place to another, and can often cause the fisherman much perplexity. Those lean and hungry fish in the barren and acid waters of some highland loch: why do they ignore, so superciliously, all that we can offer them, one day, and on another take so avidly? As for the migratory fish, why do they take our lures at all, yet so infrequently and so capriciously? Well, let us be grateful that these things are as they are. Trying to work out the answers, and acting upon our theories is what makes fishing so pleasurable an activity. If it were much easier, it would lose its savour and we would lose interest – we might as well be fishing for mackerel!

There are all sorts of ways of seeing and enjoying the countryside. My prejudice in favour of fishing stems from the fact that not only has the sport taken me to places which I would otherwise have been most unlikely to discover, but that almost invariably they have been places of exceptional beauty and interest. Water enlivens and enhances any scene; it also attracts and encourages a greater variety of life-forms, both plant and animal, than any other habitat or environment. It is, after all, vital to the survival of them all. The fisherman who is not, at least to some extent, a naturalist, misses much of the pleasure of a day's fishing, for so often there are things to be seen from the water's edge, which rival in interest even the capture of fish. And he is ideally placed to observe whatever is going on around him, moving as he does (or ought to do) as quietly, as circumspectly and as unobtrusively as that arch-exponent of his art, the heron. Often I have fished all day without setting eyes on another human being, for fishing beats, even in populous parts of the country, are frequently remote from highways and approached only by little-used tracks. The wild creatures in the area become accustomed to seeing only fishermen, and knowing them to be harmless, feel less need for flight or concealment. The fisherman, therefore, gets opportunities for watching shy

wild animals – the otter is an obvious example – which are denied to most people. He moves in an environment where nature is still supreme, and where the hand of man is least in evidence. That, to me, is as good a reason as any for going fishing.

Occupation for a winter's evening.

Mayfly Time

I spent a lot of time in Wiltshire, as a boy, without ever discovering, or even suspecting, the joys of chalk-stream fishing. I contented myself with catching the small perch and roach that abounded in my cousin's lake, unaware that the split cane rod I used for the purpose was intended for higher things. It was a master at my prep school who put me right on this score, when he saw a photograph of me holding the rod, with a perch dangling from the end of the line. Later in my boyhood I was taken, once or twice, to the River Wylye by an old gentleman who gave me my first instruction in the proper use of a fly rod and in the gentle pursuit of dry-fly fishing, but the only real memory I have retained of these excursions relates to the antique silver marrow-scoop that my companion used to examine the stomach contents of the first fish he caught. For some reason that has stayed in my mind when all else has faded, although I still have a few of the beautiful little flies, tied by himself, which he gave me.

Since those days I have often caught trout on the dry fly, from Devonshire streams, in Wales and Scotland, even, once, on the River Spey when the salmon were proving particularly uncatchable, but it was not until last summer that I returned to the lush river valleys of Wiltshire, and learnt a little about the art of dry-fly fishing in its purest form. My host, Tony, has been at the game for many years and is a very skilful fisherman, so I was in good hands. He had planned the visit to coincide with the brief period when the mayfly are on the wing, a time which varies slightly from river to river, but which generally starts during the last week of May and

continues through the first week of June and into the second. Trout, as every fisherman knows, are inordinately fond of mayfly, so the chances of catching fish were good, even for the comparative novice.

We spent the first day in a leisurely tour of the Wylye and Nadder valleys, stopping here and there to examine different stretches of river. It was a pleasant summery day and we dawdled along river banks trying to spot fish where they lay among the gently waving beds of starwort and milfoil and water crowfoot, watching for their rises and noting, where possible, the species of fly on which they were feeding. Mayflies were about in good numbers, easily recognizable by their large size and dusky wings as they came fluttering by, or sailed, like miniature yachts, along the stream. Other species of upwinged fly, such as pale wateries and medium olives, were pointed out to me by Tony. In the air they all look much the same, at first, to the untrained eye, but the experienced chalk-stream fisherman acquires the knack of recognizing many of the commoner species at a glance, just as a good bird watcher can catch a glimpse of a bird and identify it by its 'jizz': a combination of factors such as flight action, size and colour, which are unique to a particular species and can be registered in a split second.

The thing that struck me most forcibly, as we travelled from place to place, was how different in character these chalk streams were from most of the rivers with which I was familiar. A glance at the ordnance survey map will show what I mean. Look at the River Avon, south of Salisbury. It has gathered to itself the Wylye and the Bourne, the Wylye having first been swelled by the waters of the Till and Nadder, and now the Ebble joins it too. Yet it is not a great, broad river, rushing purposefully towards the sea. Rather it is a maze of convoluted channels, which meander across the valley flats, bifurcating and re-uniting with a wonderful abandon. Man has complicated the scene further, by constructing hatches and carriers to distribute the water for his own purposes. And although, for the most part, these latter works are now neglected and disused, the overall result has been to create a landscape that has kept at bay the worst excesses of the agricultural 'improver'. There are still reedy swamps and alder carrs, wildflower meadows and osier beds, and all the teeming wildlife that such habitats encourage and sustain. Not that the picture is entirely rosy, of course. Swamps have been drained and ancient meadows sprayed with herbicide, here as elsewhere, and Tony and I came across stretches of river where the gravel bed was coated with a vile, grey sludge resulting from the excessive use of artificial fertilizers. Agricultural and atmospheric pollution have also combined to reduce hatches of fly, particularly in the case of certain species which are now much less common than they once were. One has only to move away from the valleys to the slopes of the chalk downland that enclose them, to see what damage can be done by modern methods of agriculture. In my boyhood, the typical downland turf – short and springy, starred with a myriad tiny flowers and strewn with large mounds thrown up over many decades by colonies of yellow ants – was almost universal. Today much of it has been ploughed to grow corn, and where it remains as pasture it has been sprayed and levelled. One has to search hard, on lynchets and steep escarpments, to find the few remaining pockets of ancient downland.

The chalk streams owe their special character to the fact that they are spring-fed, the rainwater being stored by the porous chalk which acts as a huge sponge, releasing it only very gradually into the rivers. Fluctuations in water level, therefore, are very slight, and the water, where it is not adversely affected by pollutants, has a crystalline quality. Since the underlying soils are strongly alkaline, there is prolific plant growth, which encourages a high density of aquatic larvae upon which the trout feed and wax fat. There was a time, not very long ago, when all the trout of these parts were wild fish and so plentiful that any idea of stocking the rivers would have seemed absurd in the extreme. Today, sadly, the angling pressure is so great that stock fish are the norm, rather than the exception. This is a fact of life, with which one has to live. What I find harder to accept is the introduction, on certain stretches of chalk stream, notably on the Test, of rainbow trout; to my mind, they have no place in rivers where our indigenous species can provide all the sport any reasonable angler could require.

The second day of my visit was spent on the River Test at Longparish (where the trout, apart from an occasional stray, are all brownies) and I had the chance to put into practice some of the theory that Tony had been imparting to me the day before. It rained continuously throughout nearly the whole of the day, a steady, remorseless downpour descending from an uncompromisingly grey sky. There were three of us, Tony, Geoff and myself, though only Geoff and I were fishing, Tony having generously assumed the role of ghillie. We spent the first hour in Tony's camper, parked beside the river at the Common, drinking coffee and watching the rain-dimpled surface of the river as it swished by between tall ramparts of yellow flag and reedmace, and waited for the rise to start.

It was nearly midday before the first mayfly began to appear on the water, and soon after a

Buttercup meadows beside the River Nadder.

14

trout rose just upstream of us, and then another. The river, here beside the Common, is divided into three channels, separated by long narrow islands covered by rank vegetation. All the fishing involves wading, for the river is closely bordered either by reed beds or by trees and bushes, but it is the kindest wading that even the most geriatric fisherman could desire, with a firm and even bottom and water levels that seldom threaten to overtop waders.

I stood there, cocooned in my waterproofs, the raindrops dripping from the front of my hood, and looked out on a little world of water and reeds and grey, insubstantial horizons – it was as if I was seeing the world through the eyes of a water vole or a moorhen. The soft patter of the falling rain, and the susurrus of the swift current as it tugged at drooping flags and broken reed-heads, were all the sounds that were to be heard, apart from bird voices: the metallic notes of coots, anxious for errant young and, muted by the rain, the sweet, cascading songs of willow warblers and the more frenzied rhapsodies of reed and sedge warblers. Faintly, from some distant thicket, a cuckoo called repeatedly.

Trout were rising now in good numbers up and down the stream, and the mayfly were coming down singly, in pairs, or sometimes in little fleets. I followed the progress of one from afar as it bobbed and gyrated among the falling raindrops and the swirls and eddies of the surface currents. About 10 yards in front of me, close in to the reeds, the water boiled briefly, I caught a fleeting glimpse of a black snout and the mayfly was engulfed. I moved forward stealthily several paces and began to get out line. When I thought that my fly was reaching a spot a foot or so beyond where the trout had risen, I let it fall. It landed lightly enough, but well to the left of where I had intended it to go. I cast again, but this time it fell too far to the right, among the reeds, and in retrieving it I inevitably put the trout down. How slipshod one's casting can become as a

The River Test at the Common, Longparish.

result of chuck-and-chance-it wet-fly fishing! Here there was no room for error. The big trout were all stationed in positions where the current delivered abundant food right to their doorsteps. They had no need to exert themselves, charging off to right or left in pursuit of distant morsels. The fly had to be put down delicately and with great accuracy if one were to have any chance of hooking a fish.

Most of the early afternoon was spent refining this art, and I missed fish by every possible means. Sometimes I moved towards them too clumsily, and put them down before I even got a fly over them; frequently my fly landed short or wide of the mark; and all too often, though accurately placed, it landed with a thump that announced, as clearly as anything could, its spurious identity. On several occasions I succeeded in rising a fish, but struck too soon or failed to follow through firmly enough, and so lost it. All these faults were pointed out to me by Tony, who had already landed the first fish of the day while demonstrating the technique to Geoff.

About the middle of the afternoon I was wading up the stretch of river nearest to the Common, ruefully wondering if I was destined ever to catch a Test trout, when things suddenly came right for me. A fish rose to a mayfly somewhere near the middle of the stream. I put a fly over it several times without exciting its suspicions, but also without rising it, and then, at about the fourth cast, the fish rose greedily. I remembered to pause before striking for the second or two that is required when fishing such a large artificial, struck firmly, and it was hooked – a fish of about 1¼ pounds.

Soon after that we had a break for tea, and then moved downriver to the stretch immediately below the white, slate-roofed mansion that was once the home of that redoubtable sportsman, Colonel Peter Hawker. I started fishing at a point where the river comes together to form a kind of pool between two islands. As I was stepping gingerly down into the water I noticed a fish rise close into the bank, a little way upstream. After it had risen a second time, I put a fly over it without result, but after several more casts must have put it down, for it ceased rising. I made a mental note of its position, however, for it was a substantial fish, yellow and crowded with black spots, like a leopard.

I waded across the river, and struck off first up a backwater where trees arched and mingled their canopies overhead. The rain was still falling and big droplets fell from the branches and splashed noisily into the river. It was a rather dark and gloomy place under the weeping sky, but mayfly were still hatching and before long I had caught another trout of just over 1 pound, besides losing one which ran under a waterlogged branch on the bed of the stream. As I turned to retrace my steps, a beautiful little fly with pale yellow body and wings came fluttering towards me and settled on my shoulder. It was a yellow May dun, a species that hatches spasmodically and in small numbers, and is therefore not of great significance to the fisherman. More importantly, so far as prospects for the evening were concerned, I came across a swarm of mayfly spinners in dancing flight about the overhanging boughs of an oak tree.

The rain was easing off now, and presently a wan glow of sunlight broke through the thinning clouds and a rainbow shimmered faintly through the trees. A painted lady butterfly forsook its shelter among the reeds and took wing, and demoiselle damsel flies with iridescent bodies and fulvous or deep purple-brown wings appeared on the riverside vegetation. As the skies cleared a rosy glow spread along the western horizon and the air was full of swallows and house martins, swooping over the trees and skimming low over the water, gorging themselves on the abundant insect life.

I was moving slowly upstream, approaching a part of the river where the banks closed in to create a narrow channel through which the water came curving down in a smooth, fast surge. Scanning the water for rising fish, I looked up and noticed a mute swan that had appeared as if from nowhere and was now regarding me in a most unfriendly fashion. A goshawk, with its mad red eyes, can look as fierce as a Tartar, and an eagle as arrogant and merciless as any medieval despot, but for an expression of pure anger the male mute swan with its close-set beady black eyes, its neck taut and arched like a cobra about to strike, and its wing feathers fanned into a quivering panache above its back, is hard to beat. Even its movements through the water, as it patrols the zone around its sitting mate, have all the threat and swagger of a janissary guarding his sultan, and I had little doubt that this one's mate was somewhere nearby. However, he kept his distance, some 10 yards ahead of me, and he lost some of his dignity as he paddled madly to climb the water slide through the narrows into the pool above. I followed him with equal difficulty, for the water was both strong and deep, and once through I saw the pen swan, alert and anxious, on her great nest of reeds away to my right. The cob allowed me to pass on, contenting himself with warning hisses and baleful glares, but as soon as I was safely past he lost interest, his neck and wing feathers quickly subsided, and his graceful neck dipped under the water as he began to feed.

Meanwhile I found myself wading through very deep water, and in places had to walk on tiptoes to prevent it slopping over the tops of my waders. I was making towards the left-hand bank, in the hope of reaching shallower water, when I noticed a good trout rise off to my right, and at just the right distance for me to reach it with my fly. At the same moment I saw Geoff further upstream, near the foot bridge, playing a fish, and Tony standing near him with landing net at the ready.

At my first attempt the fly fell short, but the fish rose again as I was retrieving line; after waiting a minute or two, I re-cast, this time placing the fly, for once, precisely where I intended it should go. The fish gulped it down and the next

The house by the Test that was once the home of that redoubtable sportsman, Colonel Peter Hawker.

moment I knew I was in to a much better fish than I had so far encountered. He fought well, with powerful dashes mostly directed towards a dangerous-looking weed bed with a raft of dead weed floating above it. On each occasion I managed to turn him in time and in the end he weakened, but even then it was some minutes before I could get him to the net, for the water was not only deep (one wader was already inundated) but also flowed very strongly so that I could only hold the net steady by pointing it directly in front of me. The fish, therefore, had to be brought to the net, rather than vice versa. At last I did scoop him up, delivered the *coup de grâce*, then ploughed on until I could find a gap in the bushes through which to climb out of the river, before detaching the hook. He weighed just 2 pounds.

By the time I had emptied out my wader, wrung out my

sock, and had a cup of coffee with Tony and Geoff – who had caught two nice fish – it was drawing towards dusk. Tony was happy for us to continue fishing as long as the fish were on the rise, and I decided to return to the leopard-spotted fish that I had tried for earlier in the afternoon. Spinners were coming down the stream now in good numbers, so I changed my fly for a spent gnat pattern and made my way back to where I had started fishing. The trees were black silhouettes now, against a sky of dusky violet, and their reflections in the water seemed blacker still, though broken here and there by the glitter of surface eddies and the rings made by rising fish. Wraiths of mist hung above the sodden vegetation along the river bank, and the air was very still. Most of the swallows and martins had gone to their roosts, and a pair of bats patrolled the river in their place, but water birds were still active and the calls of moorhens and mallard resounded in the stillness up and down the river. Even the plops and splashes of rising trout seemed unnaturally loud.

I lowered myself into the river well downstream from where my fish had been, and watched the water until I was almost mesmerized by the sinuous movements of the black reflections of the reeds. Then there was a splash, and the reflections were scattered by a series of expanding silver rings. So he was still there. Very, very slowly, with infinite caution, I crept forward until I was within casting distance, released my fly from the rod ring and began to get out line. I knew that it had to be now or never and let the fly fall, soft as thistledown, on to the water. It started to float back towards me and then, with hardly any fuss, it was sucked down, and I struck.

I recognized the fish, with his close-spotted flanks – not a red spot among them – as soon as I had him in the net. He weighed 2¼ pounds and made a fitting end to the day's fishing.

Four Test trout.

The Fonthill Brook

One of the most pleasant days of that spring visit to the southern chalk country followed our visit to the Test. The weather, for a start, was a complete contrast. It was like April used to be: brilliant sunshine alternating with brief, fierce showers, only the sunny periods were hotter than they would normally be in April.

In the morning Tony and I visited Great Ridge Wood, a rare piece of surviving woodland and a paradise for the naturalist: 1,600 acres in one great block, large portions of which are made up of trees that were allowed to regenerate naturally following upon clear felling in the First World War, and which have not been managed since. To stand on the lip of the great bowl at the western end of the wood and look down on the massed canopies of these wild-grown trees was a rare experience; it was a slice of England as it might have appeared at any time in history, unsullied by any of the works of man. This was the perfect habitat for badgers and roe deer, woodcocks, adders, sparrow hawks and nightjars. We heard nightingales singing, watched Roman snails digging into the bare earth of a track in order to lay their eggs, and a marsh fritillary sunning itself at the downland edge. In one of the woodland glades we came across frog and fly orchids, and under the woodland canopy butterfly orchids, twayblade and Solomon's seal. At the top of the wood, which has a clay cap, we even found tufts of heather.

In the afternoon, Tony had business to occupy him; I was shown the way to the little brook that runs through the valley below his house, and left to my own devices. It was an afternoon of pure delight, even though I succeeded in catching but a single fish.

The Fonthill Brook is a tributary of the Nadder, and neither, I believe, can be technically described as a chalk stream. The chalk downlands encompass their valleys, but the valleys themselves are of greensand, and the water courses do not divide and ramify in the wayward fashion of true chalk streams. They have more brook-like qualities, meandering at leisure through lush meadows, but their aquatic flora is just as rich, the insect life as various and prolific, and the trout are as fat.

The brook is fed from a large artificial lake in the grounds of Fonthill House and I started off on the stretch between the lake and the point where an old stone bridge spans the stream. It was one of those warm, early summer days when nature is at its most prodigal. Every song bird up and down the valley seemed to be singing at once, the hawthorn bushes overflowed with blossom, butterflies careered over the adjoining meadows and the air was filled with the hum of insects. Bordering the stream were thick beds of reedmace and iris, and much of the water surface was covered by creamy drifts of ranunculus. Over the stream insects of many kinds and sizes performed their brief, nuptial dances, iridescent wings sparkling in the sunlight. From the wooded sides of the valley came the soporific cooing of wood pigeons and turtle doves and I think that there was hardly a moment during that afternoon when I could not hear a cuckoo calling somewhere along the valley.

Below the bridge was a wide expanse of marshy meadow-

land, full of sedges, rushes and buttercups, where newly shorn ewes were grazing with their lambs. Here I found the first mayfly of the day – I actually watched it as it struggled free from its pupal skin and I lifted it from the water on my finger as its wings were drying prior to take-off. From then on I saw mayfly pretty regularly as I walked on down the valley, though not in the quantities in which they had been present on the Test the day before. However, the trout were taking them regularly enough whenever one offered itself, so I stuck to the mayfly pattern.

It was here, in the marshy meadow, that I met and had a few words with another fisherman. He was waiting for a companion to join him, and I gathered from his perturbed expression and anxious questions as to where I was intending to fish, that they had reckoned on having this stretch to themselves. It certainly comprised the easiest fishing, as I was soon to discover, being largely free from overhanging trees, but I was happy to put his mind at rest and as soon as I announced that I intended to explore the brook downstream, he became much more genial and wished me good luck with every appearance of sincerity.

I sauntered on, casting my fly wherever a rising trout and a gap in the bushes coincided, and soon realized that this kind of fishing required different skills to those I had been practising the day before on the Test. There I had learnt the importance of casting with the rod held on a vertical axis in order to place the fly accurately on the water. Here, however, the scope for such correct actions was limited. Downstream of the marshy meadow the brook was generally bordered, at least on one side, by trees and bushes, and on the other bank were usually dense beds of tall reeds and flags. Often the gap between the overhanging branches of the trees and the tops of the reeds (which provided the cover essential if one were not to show oneself to the fish) was narrow, necessitating difficult

Casting to a wild trout in the Hatch Pool of the Fonthill Brook.

side-casting, with the constant danger of hooking either tree or reed while getting out sufficient line. Even if one succeeded in getting through a series of false casts without mishap, and landing one's fly on the water, the chances of it coming down in just the right place were, for me at least, slim. There was one fish that I particularly wanted to attract, for I could see him quite clearly where he lay above a patch of shingle in the lee of a big clump of weed, and I had watched him come up to the surface and suck down a passing mayfly. He was a good fish for a small brook, being certainly a pound or over (these were all genuinely wild fish), and despite several bodged attempts at covering him, he kept on rising. In the end I did succeed in getting my fly to float right over his nose, but he treated it with contempt, as if quite aware of all the frantic efforts I had been making to entrap him, and then added insult to injury by rising fiercely at the first natural fly to come along. At my next attempt I embedded my fly in an alder twig, and having had to wade into the stream in order to retrieve it, I acknowledged defeat, deciding that unless some extremely deft angler came long, that trout had a very good chance of living out the summer.

Another fish that gave me a lot of trouble was lying close into the far bank, just downstream of a large tree root that projected into the water. Here I had more room to cast, but the difficulty was to drop the fly in the very small space between the root and where the fish was rising. Although the current swirled around the root, carrying natural food to the fish, I found that drag from the line prevented the artificial from doing the same thing if placed upstream of the root, pulling it instead away from the fish and towards the middle of the stream. I did manage at least to rise this fish, by letting my fly fall on to the tree root itself and thence, by means of a series of small twitches, into the water. It gathered way, was taken by the current, and sailed over the fish which rose to it readily, but although I felt the contact, the hook – no doubt through some fault of timing in the strike – failed to bite home.

Problems such as these kept me pleasantly occupied for an hour or so, then the skies began to darken and presently the rain came teeming down; since I had come out without waterproofs I was forced to flee to the shelter of a large oak tree in the adjoining meadow. I leant against its hard, furrowed trunk, smoked a pipe and looked out through a veil of raindrops as the features of the landscape became blurred by the deluge and every leaf and grass stem trembled under its impact. The downpour lasted only a short time and ended as quickly as it had begun, tailing off into a scatter of droplets that suddenly sparkled as the dark clouds melted away and the sun shone out again from a sky of pristine blue. Everything was steaming and, as I walked on down the meadow, there was a rainbow-hued glitter in the tall grass and a delicious exhalation of flowery scents.

I came to a lovely little round pool, known as the Hatch Pool, where the water came rippling in between mossy stanchions of ochreous stone. Here, for once, there was room to cast freely, and by wading up the fast, shallow stream at the tail of the pool, I was able to command most of its area. Several fish were rising in the pool. I chose one on the far side and aimed towards it the ginger-hackled, raffia-bodied fly with pheasant-herl tails that Tony had tied for me and which, though it bore only a slight resemblance to a mayfly in my eyes, had done good execution among the Test trout the day before. This fish was equally gullible and took the fly at the first cast. After a short, sharp battle, during which it dashed about the pool and put down all the other fish, I got it over the net – a fish of about ¾ pound – but disengaged the hook without lifting it from the water, since we were already well supplied with trout. It darted off, no doubt a wiser fish, and I hoped, rather ungenerously so far as my fellow anglers were concerned, that in future it might be less easily deluded.

I wandered on for perhaps another half-mile, and after crossing a farm track, came to a meadow, the lower part of which, beside the brook, was a mass of southern marsh orchids. The bright magenta flowers were scattered among buttercups, water mint, horsetails and a variety of sedges and rushes, and I had never before seen this species growing in such profusion or with such tall, many-flowered spikes. There were spotted orchids there as well, recognizable by their blotched leaves, the flowers still in bud.

I tried for several more trout without success, but at last a careless chuck fixed my fly firmly in a high willow branch where there was no chance of reaching it, and I was forced to haul on the line until the fine 5X leader parted. While I sat on the ground beside the stream, choosing and tying on a fresh fly, a herd of crossbred bullocks spied me across the meadow, and came lumbering down the hill towards me. At a distance of about 5 yards they formed a semi-circle behind me, blowing softly through their noses, ears twitching, tails a-swish, treacly brown eyes all directed towards me in bovine wonderment. Then, slowly, they began to jostle their way forward again, and the air around me was pervaded by their sweet, milky, farmyard smell. The boldest of them was curling his rough, pink tongue, evidently intent on testing me for taste, when I shooed them away, but they only flounced back a yard or so and when I began fishing again, they all followed me to the bank and watched the proceedings with mournful expressions, like a bevy of expert anglers sadly contemplating an inept student. After some five minutes they lost interest, and one by one they moved away and started to graze.

Soon after, the sky began to darken once more, and this time, when the shower came, I waded into the brook and sheltered under a tangled overhang made up of alder, hazel, bramble and dog rose, which was thick enough to keep me nearly dry as the rain pelted down.

Again, I had that feeling of my surroundings being reduced and contracted into a microcosm. The outside, workaday

A situation familiar to every fisherman: young cattle are very inquisitive.

24

world seemed far away and unreal, the near landscape an indistinct blur in vertically hatched shades of green and grey. Only objects near at hand had tangible properties and I became acutely aware of twigs strung with trembling rain-drops, glistening leaves, strands of spiders' gossamer and the deep crimson thorns on an arching stem of briar. The water at my feet passed swiftly by but the contours on its surface remained almost constant, endlessly repeating the same elaborate patterns, varied only by the overlapping and expanding rings of the falling rain. The sound of the rain drumming and pattering on the foliage above my head and the mesmeric qualities of the moving water combined with the snugness of my bosky shelter, inducing a state of contemplative lethargy which was very pleasant: I was almost sorry when the sun broke out once more and the rain moved away down the valley, leaving only a fragile rainbow to mark its passing.

By this time there were few fly hatching and the fish seemed to have lost interest, so I began to wend my way slowly back up the valley. It had been a most enjoyable afternoon, though I did wish that my only fish had been one of those tricky customers for which I had tried so hard, instead of that rather easy fish from the Hatch Pool.

Chalk-stream kingfisher.

September on the Test

The freshness, the orderliness, the vivid colours of early summer had passed away. Now the leaves that hung in ponderous trusses over the river were sombre-hued, leathery in texture, defaced by scars and galls and eaten away by caterpillars. The riverside vegetation was tangled and sered by summer sun and storms, and out of it tall seed heads arose, of hogweed, hemp agrimony and hemlock, to which clusters of thistledown and fluffy willow seeds adhered. Though the predominant colours were greens and browns, there were also the yellows of fleabane and orange balsam and shades of pink, mauve and purple were provided by willowherb, thistles and hempnettle, marsh woundwort and water mint. The velvety purple-brown heads of reedmace and the tall magenta spikes of loosestrife lent a special richness to the scene, and the whole atmosphere was one of rioting abundance, of ripeness and fecundity, as plants strove with each other for a share of the sunlight to ripen their fruits, and insects, in countless numbers, garnered the last nectar from the late blooms.

It was mid-September. I had driven down to Hampshire by way of crowded motorways, and it had been an immense relief to leave the hideous stream of frantic, hurtling traffic, and suddenly to find myself driving along country lanes and through quiet villages, with delectable glimpses, every now and then, of the river away to my right. I found Tony at the Common, where he was standing, hands on hips, beside the river, peering over the tops of the reeds at the water surface with that concentrated gaze that marks the dry-fly fisherman.

He greeted me, as I joined him on the bank, with the information that there were plenty of blue-winged olives hatching, and for five minutes or so we stood together watching the smooth, swift flow of the river, the rings of rising trout and the occasional olive coming down with the current while others fluttered by, always in an upstream direction. Behind us, on the road, was Tony's camper, which was to be our headquarters for the three days of my visit, saving us daily journeys to and from his home in Wiltshire.

'Well, let's get going,' said Tony presently, 'no point in hanging about.' We tackled up, and ten minutes later we were wading together up the far arm of the river, from the bridge, through shallows at first, where shoals of grayling scattered and darted past our feet, then into deeper water where a rising trout gave me my first opportunity, but spurned my clumsily presented fly. A little further on, leaning out over the river from the far bank, was a vast old alder tree whose canopy of dark leaves hung like a great crinoline over the water, and 20 yards beyond that the river divided again, both arms eventually disappearing from sight among forests of reeds. When we came level with the tree, we stopped to take stock. 'There's a nice trout,' said Tony, after a pause. 'Look, he's lying over that golden patch of gravel, just in front of the alder tree – and by Jove! there's an even better fish beyond him; now that's a really good fish!' I strained my eyes to pierce the amber depths beneath the glancing reflections of light on the water's surface, and presently made out first one, then the other fish. The furthest of the two certainly was a nice fish, Tony reckoned a possible 2-pounder, but both were lying

motionless as logs of wood, and took no notice even when a struggling fly was borne by the current directly over them.

'We'd better leave them be for the present,' said Tony. 'They'll still be there another time; at the moment they're not interested in feeding. The problem's going to be getting a fly over the big'un, without scaring the smaller one.' He scratched his head and pondered for a moment. 'Ah, well, let's give 'em a wide berth and try up here for now. Look, there's a decent trout rising over there, see? Just this side of where that broken reed's trailing in the water.'

We continued our slow upstream progress and I soon concluded that these September trout were an altogether different proposition from their ingenuous brethren of the mayfly season. Using a much smaller fly, one had to be quicker on the strike, but the chief problem lay in rising the fish in the first place. Big trout that had survived a whole season were educated to a high degree and not easily taken in by imitations. The fly had to be perfectly presented if there were to be any chance of deceiving them, and even so there were plenty of fish which consistently ignored any but the real thing.

Later in the afternoon we moved down below Colonel Hawker's house where Tony, who had some visits to make, left me to fish alone. I fished the broad stretch below the foot bridge, and although I caught no trout, I did catch my first Test grayling and hooked and lost two others. The grayling is a curious fish. It is a member of the *Salmonidae*, and sports the characteristic adipose fin, but in other respects it bears little resemblance to any of the *Salmo* species. Its most peculiar feature is the huge, beautifully marked and coloured dorsal fin, and although the grayling is less renowned as a fighter than the trout, it can use this fin to advantage when hooked, hoisting it like a great lugsail, and cutting across the current in

Trout rising to a blue-winged olive beneath the trailing leaves of an alder.

sharp dashes which sometimes end by jerking the hook from its hold. Its sparsely spotted, silvery-grey body is marked by zigzag longitudinal stripes, and it has a forked tail, pointed snout and slightly underhung jaw. It was not until early in the nineteenth century that it was introduced to the River Test from the Avon, a day bitterly rued by some, for there are many trout anglers who loathe the grayling. Others appreciate the sport which, being a spring spawner, it provides during the winter months, as well as enjoying its delicate flavour. Tony and I had fried grayling the next evening for our supper, and I took several home with me. My own opinion, for what it is worth, is that the grayling makes at least as good eating as any trout, and that its presence in a river is a bonus rather than a disadvantage. I am prejudiced, no doubt, by the fact that on this occasion the grayling gave me some sport which, had it been left to the trout, I would have been largely denied.

We camped that evening on an extensive grass ley beside an avenue of beeches on a neighbouring estate, and the next morning, after a leisurely breakfast and a long walk with my young dog, we returned to the river. Once again we started at the Common, wading up from the bridge towards the big alder tree. Tony wanted me to have a try for the large trout that we had seen the day before, but I persuaded him that I would rather, on this occasion, be a spectator. The two trout were stationed just as they had been, the larger one a yard or so beyond the smaller, both of them 2 or 3 yards upstream from where the alder boughs dipped towards the water. We had made our approach as stealthily as possible, and now stood quietly regarding them, hoping that one of them would rise to a passing fly, for blue-winged olives were about in plenty, both in the air and on the water. I suppose we had stood there nearly ten minutes, during which time neither fish had stirred a fin, when Tony decided that he would give it a try anyway – if they were put down, there would always be another chance later in the day or the next morning. The cast had to be made obliquely across the river, and it was vital to get the fly directly over the big fish, without lining or otherwise alarming the smaller one. This Tony succeeded in doing, but the Sherry Spinner sailed overhead without eliciting any response and was gently retrieved from under the boughs of the alder.

'Blast!' said Tony quietly. 'I think I'll see if I can't give him something that'll wake him up – surprise him into action. I'll take this fly off, and put on a thumping big sedge – see if that'll do the trick.'

The sedge flew out as neatly and accurately as the Sherry Spinner had done, and once again I held my breath. Then there was an eruption on the water's surface and Tony's old cane rod bent into an arc. 'Got him!' he said with satisfaction, as the reel sang and the line cut through the water. The fish fought splendidly, running downstream and across the river first, then back and under the hanging boughs of the alder. Several times Tony coaxed him away from the dangerous, hidden roots of the tree, and each time he returned, forcing Tony to hold the rod low over the water, sometimes with the tip below the surface. Eventually he made another run across the stream, and this time Tony was able to follow him and reel in line. He tried to get back but did not have the strength, and presently he came weaving over the net and was lifted from the water. He weighed only a little over 1½ pounds, but he was a handsome fish, deep and shapely, with a saffron-yellow belly and large scarlet spots along his lovely burnished golden flanks.

It was a beautiful day, in a summer notorious for the paucity of beautiful days – balmy, soft, with a gentle upstream breeze and a milky blue sky across which fleecy clouds drifted in little flocks. We spent most of the afternoon on the reach above the Common, where the river winds between long islands and borders of reedy marshland that are enclosed by tall, wooded cliffs, giving it an air of seclusion and mystery. Chiffchaffs were singing everywhere, up and down the river, ghosts of spring. They stay behind when other warblers have

Tony netting out his trout by the big alder tree.

gone, taking advantage of the lack of competition and feeding up on the abundant insect life before commencing their own journey south. As Tony and I were wading up a long stretch of shallows, after parking the camper on the cliff-top, a kingfisher flashed past us in a dazzle of blue fire, and then a sparrow hawk flew over the reeds to our left.

We came to a bend in the river where the water was deeper, and where the dark reflections from the wooded slopes cut the surface glare and gave us a clear view of the underwater landscape – the forests of starwort and ranunculus and glades of gravel and silt, and the fish that moved in lazy shoals among them, or lay with gently fanning pectoral fins beneath favourable currents, waiting for succulent morsels to come their way. We moved foward slowly, a few careful paces at a time, and occasionally (Tony was not fishing) I cast to a rising fish. Two more grayling came to the net but the trout still eluded me. Indeed, many of them were apparently replete, and uninterested in the few fly that were now coming down the river. But it was an absorbing experience, a chance to observe fish behaviour in a panoramic setting, which is seldom vouchsafed to any but the chalk stream angler.

We returned to the camper for a cup of tea at about five o'clock, and sat for a long time chatting idly, looking down at the river below us and listening to the river sounds – the hum of insects, the calls and twitterings of birds and the occasional 'plop' of a rising fish. The sun was warm, and induced a state of soporific inertia.

At the approach of evening the whole scene was bathed in a golden light, and fly began to hatch in considerable numbers. In a surprisingly short time all the ambient air was full of them; they were as thick as snowflakes and they glowed in the sunlight like sparks from a bonfire. I had never seen anything like it before. However, when we had gathered our gear and clambered down the steep bank to the river, there were still very few fly on the water. We waded upriver again, this time beyond the bend where we had stopped before, and soon we

were both fishing hard, totally absorbed.

That was an unforgettable evening; the only trout I hooked (apart from a very small one which was returned to the water) shook itself free of the hook after boring into a tangle of ranunculus stems, but two more grayling went into the creel and Tony also had several grayling, besides a trout of just over a pound – a pretty and unusual fish whose flanks had a greenish-blue iridescence under their close covering of black and blood-red spots. The huge concourse of ephemerids that filled the air above and around us, attracted a great throng of swallows and house martins which swooped and weaved above the water, making the most of the feast that had been provided for them. There were bats about also; some that flew very close above the water, frequently taking insects from the surface, were, I suspect, Daubenton's bats. We saw the sparrow hawk again, flying across the river and back down over the reed beds; very soon after that the swallows and martins behind us all came together in a twittering, excited mass, and at the same moment I saw a hawk slicing between the tree-tops, at the summit of the cliff to our right. I thought for a moment that it was another sparrow hawk, but then I realized from its speed and long, sickle wings that it was a hobby. It plummetted down among the panicking hirundines, but the end of its raking stoop was hidden from me by trees at the bend of the river, so I could not see whether or not it had taken out a bird. However, it did not re-appear, so I suspect that it had.

As the sun dipped behind the trees and the glow of evening took on deeper and richer tones, the river became a shimmering sheet of bronze where it lay in the path of the sun's low beams. The light breeze had dropped away to virtually nothing, and in the still reaches the velvety dark reflections of the trees were almost leaf-perfect. Sounds were magnified: a water vole crunching and rustling among the flags, the harsh, cranking cries of a pair of herons that laboured overhead, pheasants 'cocking up' in the woods, the clucks of moorhens,

and, most eery of all, the long, trilling calls of little grebes.

Despite the great hordes of fly in the air, the fall of spinners had not been great, and although grayling and a few trout were still rising here and there, we turned to retrace our steps when the red orb of the sun sank behind the sallow bushes in the west. The sky was still lit by a dusky orange glow, and as we waded down the stream, there was a continuous criss-crossing overhead of small flights of mallard and pochard. The sibilant whisper of their wings, getting louder and then receding, followed us all the way back, and soon it was joined by the slower wing beats and high-pitched cries of Canada geese, as skein after skein flew past us down the river. All were making for the wide pool that lay directly opposite where the camper was parked, and by the time we had climbed out of the river and were hauling ourselves up the steep bank, the sound of their clamorous cries and the deep thrumming of their wings, as they broke formation and parachuted or side-slipped down to join their companions on the water, made a glorious cacophony.

Back at our campsite under the beeches we sipped our whiskies as a brace of grayling crackled and hissed in the pan, and talked over the day's events, as fishermen will. Outside, the loom of the downland and the humped shapes of distant beech copses lay black beneath a sky of deep violet in which a myriad stars twinkled. We felt pleasantly tired, and at peace with the world.

The last day of my visit was warm but overcast. In the morning a rather stiff downstream breeze made casting more difficult, but it dropped away in the afternoon. We spent the whole day on the upper water, where we had finished the day before, or rather I did, for Tony did not join me until mid-afternoon.

'Any luck?' he called, as he emerged out of the reeds, having walked up the lane and come down through the wood.

Fishing the evening rise on the River Test above the Common.

'Only grayling,' I shouted back. 'There don't seem to be any trout about any more, and those I have seen all seem to be on hunger-strike.'

He lowered himself into the river and waded across to join me. In front of us was quite a large area of broken water which ended abruptly some 10 yards ahead. Beyond that was a long glassy stretch in which patches of weed lay like green archipelagoes. Only dimples, cat's-paws and miniature swirls betrayed the swift movement of the water beneath the mirror calm of its surface.

After a while Tony spoke again. 'There are your trout,' he said, pointing towards the far edge of the broken water, 'plenty of them. They're nymphing, that's why they wouldn't look at your fly.' And there they were, little arrowing wakes, boils on the surface, difficult to see in the choppy water, but clear enough once they had been pointed out. Tony lent me a Pheasant-tail Nymph with which to replace my Lunn's Particular and I was soon in action. The Nymph has to be put down firmly, rather than being floated down like a dry fly, but I soon got the hang of that and by this time, after all the practice I had had, I was placing the fly with a fair degree of accuracy. None the less the trout did not take. Whatever they were feeding on, it was presumably something which was not well imitated by my Pheasant-tail. I hooked another grayling, and began to take a slightly more jaundiced view of that accommodating species. Time was getting on, for I had planned to leave for home by 4.30 and it was already nearly four o'clock, but then I got a good, firm take, and soon my line was zipping through the water in a manner that left me in no doubt that there was a trout at the end of it. It was only a fish of about ¾ pound, as it turned out, and I sent it back with an admonition to grow bigger, but I had caught my September trout at last, and it rounded off nicely my three days on this fairest and most bountiful of trout rivers.

33

West Country Streams

Cultivation has been nibbling away at the edges of Exmoor for many years. In consequence the area of wild moorland has been much reduced, but none the less, if you park your car on one of the high, windswept roads that traverse the heart of the moor, and strike out across country, it is surprising how quickly you can leave behind the tourist traffic and almost every other vestige of human activity. Only the hardy, black-faced sheep that crop the moorland grasses and weave narrow, winding paths through bracken and heather, indicate man's active management of the environment.

Wherever you walk on the moor, sooner or later the land will fall away, leading you down to a green valley of rushes and close-cropped turf where a tiny stream of clear though peat-stained water brawls and babbles over its stony bed. I love these little rills, for they are like great rivers in miniature, complete with pools and runs, glides and stickles, gorges and cascades. The fingerling trout that inhabit them are like scaled-down salmon, and stunted hawthorns and sallow bushes take the place of great oaks and elms upon their banks.

Running northwards towards the Bristol Channel, these insignificant streams collect water from the hills, unite with one another and swell in size until they become first brooks, then rivers in their own right. For the last few miles before they spill into the sea they plunge down off the moor through steep-sided combes clothed in natural oak woodland. Here the oaks, beeches and feathery ashes arch and mingle their

Heron: paradigm of the patient angler.

branches above the stream, and shafts of light come slanting down to strike sparks of amber fire from the pebble beds of shallow runs and to kindle an unearthly green glow in the deep, black pools gouged out by waterfalls. The sound of the rushing, falling water fills the valleys, as it has done unceasingly for countless centuries, a gentle babble in warm summer weather when the river runs low, rising to a roaring diapason in times of spate.

It was on the East Lyn river – a fairly tranquil stretch where it runs along the lip of Exmoor before commencing its precipitous descent towards the sea – that I first experienced the delights of Devon fishing. The trout were small – seldom better than three to a pound – but plump, beautifully spotted and wild as could be. I fished for them with a small brook rod and a dry fly and the sport called for some cunning casting and very fast reactions, in both of which respects I was often deficient. But what matter? The pursuit was all-engrossing and the surroundings as timelessly lovely as any to be found in England.

A decade or more was to pass before, in 1977, I found myself again in Devonshire with a fishing rod. This time our destination was a larger river, the Torridge, which rises very near the coast at Buck's Cross and flows far inland before describing a great loop and heading once more towards the sea at Bideford. We stayed at Sheepwash, at a fishing hotel which is comfortable and welcoming, with excellent food and well-kept beer – a model for all such places. It was a quiet place, secluded from the main tourist routes, where we would

An infant river on Exmoor: the Farley Water.

wake in the morning to the sound of cows crossing the village square on their way to be milked, and the rattle of milk churns, a once familiar country sound that is gone forever.

On that first visit we devoted most of our energies to the pursuit of salmon, but I have to say that neither then nor on any of three subsequent visits to the river have I seen a Torridge salmon – or any hint of one – alive, and only one dead. The Torridge was once a famous salmon fishery, and the downriver beats in particular, such as Undercleave, Chapel and Madeira, seemed such perfect salmon waters that it never occurred to us to fish for anything else. One day we had the chance to fish one of the loveliest beats, at Brimblecombe, where a steep descent through woodland led to an enchanted valley, the meadows bordering the river brilliant with wild flowers and alive with butterflies. I remember Charlie reading aloud from an old book he had borrowed on the Torridge fishery, which contained statements such as 'this pool always holds 20-25 salmon', and wondering why we saw no sign of a fish. We did not realize, at that time, the scale of the deterioration in the salmon runs, and such decline as was admitted seemed mainly to be attributed to netting at sea and in the estuary. It is only in very recent years that the state of the Torridge has become a national, even an international, issue and we now know that although netting activities are undoubtedly a significant factor, the chief cause of the declining runs of migratory fish is pollution: pollution from sewage, from industry, from silage seepage and farm slurry, and from agricultural fertilizers and their concomitant, the over-stocking of pastures bordering the river, with the consequent increase in organic and chemical run-off. Some action is now, at last, being taken to clean up the river, and more is promised, but it is a scandal and a cause for despair that governmental and bureaucratic indifference should have allowed the situation to become so dire before those responsible could be kicked into doing something about it. Even now the voices of the riparian owners and rod fishers carry little weight in the argument and any action that is taken will be on behalf of cleaner drinking water and less foul beaches for the tourists. That a river should be saved from death for its own sake and that of all the wild creatures that depend on it, irrespective of special interests and the profit motive, does not seem to figure in the mind of government. It is as if, for these people, whether in Whitehall or in local government offices, it is enough that the river should flow prettily through its rural setting, with its old stone bridges and tree-lined banks, providing picturesque glimpses for passing tourists from their car windows. From a hundred yards away, the deadest of rivers can look attractive as its waters glitter in the sunlight, and with any luck the wind will carry the stench of sewage and chemicals and rotting fish carcasses in another direction. But of course pollution is a cumulative and progressive evil. The fish may be the first to suffer, but next it will be the turn of the otters, the herons, kingfishers and dippers, the aquatic plant life, and the insects and other creatures that depend on it for their larval stages. Unfortunately, there are all too many people who would recognize nothing amiss if the fauna were reduced to nothing but sparrows and rabbits and the flora to grass and daisies, and who would care little even if the true situation were explained to them. Their children would have to contract typhoid from the drinking water before their screams of protest would be heard. Were this not the case, public indignation would have pressurized the government into cleaning up our rivers and coastal waters and attacking the root causes of acid rain and all other forms of pollution long since.

One encouraging sign, following the start of the clean-up process, has been that although salmon stocks have remained at a low level, the run of sea-trout in the Torridge last year was the best for many years, and after that first visit, it was to sea-trout and brown trout that we turned for our sport.

Several of the Sheepwash beats are stocked with trout and one can have good sport, particularly on the dry fly, with fish of between 1 and 2 pounds. On the uppermost beats the fish are mostly wild, and though they seldom exceed ½ pound, can give equally exciting sport, so long as one uses sufficiently light tackle.

Our first visit to the river was made in April and although, as I have already mentioned, we wasted a lot of time fishing, with both fly and spinner, for non-existent salmon, we did finally turn our attention to the brownies.

At that time of year the colours along the river are full of subtlety. Summer's almost overpowering array of rich, dark greens is yet to come; instead there are creamy yellows, ochres and umbers and rusty reds. The shades of green are the most delicate imaginable and there are washes of purple in the budding crowns of the alders, and flecks of orange and pink from the swelling buds of sycamore and field maple. The reeds and flags along the riverside mingle sharp green spears of new growth with ragged brown relicts from the previous year, and on the river banks are drifts of wild daffodils nodding their saffron heads in the breeze.

I caught my first Torridge trout from the stickle at the head of a pool called Jack White's Pit – named, I believe, after an old Torridge angler who died there and was found some hours later with one salmon on the bank beside him and another in the water, still attached to his line. Could anyone conceive of a better way for a fisherman to go? There was a hatch of large dark olives, but no trout were rising and consequently I was fishing wet with a Gold-ribbed Hare's Ear.

I remember that fish – which was a nice pounder – particularly well, because my attention was diverted, while I was playing it, by the reeling song of a grasshopper warbler that suddenly started up from the plantation across the river. As a result I nearly lost it when it ran among some roots under the bank. The line was momentarily snagged and I expected a break, but when I managed to free it, the fish, to my surprise,

was still there, and was duly brought to the net. I remember, too, another fish, from my next year's visit which was made several weeks later in the year, in early May. It was a large fish, around 1¾ pounds, which kept rising at the tail of Alder Island Pool; I tried for it several times on the first day and again later in the week, using a variety of different patterns, both wet and dry, all of which were ignored. On the last day of my visit I had the Wooda beat again, and there he was, still rising regularly in the same spot. This time I made my approach very cautiously, and from a kneeling position behind some bank-side cover, put a dry Coachman over him and was taken immediately. He was the best brownie I have had from the Torridge, and gave a good account of himself, but I was almost sorry as I lifted him on to the bank: I felt I had established a rather personal relationship with him, and it seemed a shame to interrupt a life of such epicurean contentment. Alas, greed, or maybe curiosity (for the Coachman with its fat body of peacock herl and white wings is an unlikely looking fly), overcame discernment at the end.

An early August visit to the river, a year or two later, was particularly notable, for me, for the large number of silver-washed fritillaries that were fluttering over the river-side vegetation or flying high over the river and settling in the tops of the oak trees, and the hordes of demoiselle damsel flies with their iridescent emerald or sapphire bodies and cinnamon wings, which in older specimens would deepen to indigo or purple. On that occasion it was my companion, Mike, who had most of the fishing success, catching eight or nine fish up to 1¾ pounds. I had to be content mainly with smaller, wild trout, but caught the only sea-trout of the week, a fish of 1¼ pounds, taken from a fast run on the Rockhay beat, on a dark and windy night.

My most recent visit to the Torridge – this year, 1988 –

The River Taw near Umberleigh: John fishing the run down to the Hurdle Pool.

consisted of a couple of days' fishing on May 18th and 19th. The water was low and dirty after a long period of drought, but mayfly were already hatching in good numbers. I had forgotten to bring any mayfly patterns with me, but a large fly of uncertain identity that I happened to have in my box, with grey hackles and a yellowish ribbed body, seemed to answer as well, and I caught a stock fish on the first day and seven wild brownies on the second.

From Sheepwash I went on to the River Taw which, like the Torridge, runs into Bideford Bay, and met up with a friend, John, who was making a slight detour on his way from Essex to a wedding in Dorset. The Taw is yet another beautiful river which ought to be more productive than is currently the case. We fished a beat that lies between Umberleigh and the junction with the River Mole, and although the low water did not give us ideal fishing conditions, there was compensation in the brilliance and warmth of the weather. Every moment of those days was a delight, whether wading the fast streams in the heat of the day, lying on flowery banks to eat our lunch, or fishing far into the moonlit hours when the river became a ghostly, whispering thoroughfare of spangled silvery lights and Stygian shadows under the overhanging limbs of the great oak trees on its banks.

Making one's way along the banks, one caught the scent of may blossom and of tansy and wild garlic; in the muddy shallows yellow flag irises were coming into flower and from rocks in the stream grew huge clumps of shiny-leaved wild celery. On open banks the meadow flowers grew in galaxies of bright colour: pink lady's-smock, purple-blue bugle, the vivid yellows of buttercup and hay rattle, daisies, speedwell and cranesbill; while in shadier parts, among the boles of mighty oaks and ashes, alders and sycamores and bushes of hawthorn and hazel, there were bluebells and red campion and great drifts of lilac-flowered *Montia*, mixed with the starry white flowers of ransoms. Butterflies were everywhere, mainly peacocks, orange-tips, brimstones and speckled woods, and

over the river ephemerids performed their nuptial dances – mayflies, olives, a few March browns and other species that I could not identify. Some of them, landing on the water to lay their eggs or, as spinners, to die, provided meals for hungry trout and parr; others, still airborne, fell prey to swallows and swifts, house martins and sand martins that weaved and swooped in mazy flight all along the river, or to the grey and pied wagtails, wrens, warblers and many other kinds of bird that were rearing families beside the stream. In shallow water at the river's edge, I was glad to note healthy colonies of frog tadpoles, black as spilt ink, that swayed together with the movement of the water.

With such a rich variety of flora and fauna all around, it seemed that only the river itself was providing a less than perfect environment for its denizens. That there were salmon in it was proved by the fact that the night before our arrival a party of poachers had been caught red-handed netting the Junction Pool where the River Mole joins the Taw. They had taken half a dozen fish which were still in the net, and alive, when they were interrupted, and fortunately the River Bailiff was in time to return the salmon unharmed to the water. The fact that we caught no salmon of course proves nothing, particularly as the prevailing low water conditions were not very

Sedge warbler and yellow flag irises.

propitious, and similarly our lack of success at night has no bearing on whether or not the early run of large sea-trout was under way. But we saw no fish move apart from one – whether salmon or sea-trout we could not be sure – which rose consistently under the low boughs of an oak tree in the largest and stillest of the pools, and somehow we got the feeling – perhaps quite mistaken – that few were in the water. That brown trout were scarce there was little doubt, for risers were few and far between despite the abundance of fly. I foul-hooked one on wet fly at the end of a pool, but as I drew it tail-first towards the net, it gave a wriggle and freed itself. Soon after I noticed another rising further back up the pool, in some fast water near the opposite bank, and changing to my dry-fly rod, with the grey-hackled fly that had proved successful on the Torridge, I cast a long line across the pool, was taken, and presently landed it – a fish of about 11 inches. That was the only success of our two days on the Taw.

Approaching the river each day, we had to cross a single-track railway that ran parallel with the river, by means of a level crossing. On the outermost of the two stout oak gates that guarded the crossing was a heavy iron plate on which were embossed in large capital letters the words: 'PENALTY FOR NOT SHUTTING THE GATE, £2'. Each time I saw it, it gave me a twinge of nostalgia for the days when such an assurance of the permanence and stability of things could be so confidently indulged. What, I wondered, would have been the outcome of our two days' fishing, in the year when that plate was bolted to the gate? When steam trains still chugged along the line, stopping at every tiny halt, when traffic on the roads was sparse and the farmlands bordering the river had not yet been subjected to the huge concentration of artificial fertilizer and drenchings with insecticide and fungicide and a host of other noxious chemicals, as was now the case.

Before leaving I called on the river's lady proprietor to pay for our fishing, and talked, over a cup of coffee, to an elderly gentleman who had fished the river all his life. He told me of

Demoiselle damsel flies.

41

country which have deteriorated alarmingly over the last few decades, but they face not only the inexorable problems of increasing population and urbanization and the seemingly irreversible trends in farming practice, but forces of greed, inertia and ignorance which sometimes make it very hard to be optimistic for the future.

Southern marsh orchids at mayfly time.

days when it was nothing unusual to fish the beat down from top to bottom in the course of a morning, picking up six salmon on the way, and hanging them in trees to be out of the way of otters and crows until they could be collected on the way back; when the boulders on the river bed were not coated in chemical slime and brown trout were legion. In retrospect the old days always seem better, but in this case I think there can be little doubt that they truly were. Today there are people working very hard to try to reverse the decline of these magnificent West Country rivers and others around the

A Handful of Rivers

The wise fisherman, travelling about the country, will generally have a rod in his car, and a minimal supply of fishing gear, even if fishing is not the prime purpose of his journey, for one can never be sure when an opportunity may arise to fish an unfamiliar water. Such serendipitous encounters seldom result, at least in my experience, in notable baskets, but exploring a new piece of water is always a pleasure, and if one succeeds in catching a fish or two, that is a bonus.

Fishermen are naturally jealous of their fishing, so that an outright invitation to a stranger to fish the local water is an uncommon occurrence. It did happen to me once, though, when I was on my way home from a visit to the Western Isles, and made a detour to call at Wigtown in Galloway. Admittedly I was acquainted with several of the locals, having been there wildfowling in past winters, but none the less I was surprised when one of the farmers whose land bordered the saltmarshes, and who was in the bar at the hotel that evening, offered me his rod on the River Cree for the following day. I explained that I had been trouting, and had no salmon rods with me, whereupon the local bank manager said he would lend me one, and sure enough, when I turned up at his bank the next morning, there was not only the rod, but a landing net of optimistic proportions and a selection of flies awaiting me. Such generosity is rare indeed and although I did not catch a Cree salmon, I had a most enjoyable day on the river.

An equally fortuitous set of circumstances led to an afternoon's fishing on the River Lugg in Herefordshire, a long time ago. I remember the occasion well, for two reasons. First, because, despite being at that time a very inexperienced fisherman, I caught my first grayling, fishing dry with a Red Tag. Quite a good fish, too, at well over a pound in weight. Second, because the scene had a timeless quality and a profound 'Englishness' that put one in mind of Elgar symphonies, Victorian watercolours and the writings of Francis Brett Young. It was a warm and almost windless September day of mellow sunshine and slow-drifting, fleecy cloudlets. Cattle and sheep munched their way across the pastures bordering the river, there was the all-pervasive hum of insects and the aromatic scent of bonfire smoke hung on the air. On the river banks the hawthorn bushes glowed with clusters of crimson berries, and yellow leaves fluttered down from the willows to float, with drifts of thistledown, along the stream. Often, little parties of mallard, the drakes still in their dull eclipse plumage, would rise quacking as I rounded a bend in the river, and a family of mute swans sailed past me, the cob fanning his wing coverts and glaring at me with his beady black eyes as he went by. On one side of the river were flat pasturelands; on the other parkland sloped gently upwards to where, in a commanding position and surrounded by venerable trees, there stood a grey stone mansion with shuttered windows and a sad air of neglect, that faced blindly out across the village and the broad ribbon of the Wye, towards the distant mountains of Wales. Downstream of me was the village: old red brick houses and stone barns, the church of rusty red sandstone with its squat tower and

shallow steeple, and the ancient many-arched bridge with its great sloping buttresses beneath which the Lugg flowed on its way to join the Wye, a short distance below. This year I visited the river again, to make the drawing that accompanies this chapter. It was May, rather than September, and the hawthorns were covered with creamy blossom, but I was glad to see that the scene remained largely unchanged. Long may it remain so.

Another river to which I have made several brief visits is the Teifi, in Carmarthenshire. On the first occasion, I was with a falconer friend who was flying his hawks in the hills that rise behind the small market town of Llanybydder. On the road up to the hills was a large rubbish tip where there was often a huge concourse of ravens, together with carrion crows and jackdaws. The ravens sometimes numbered over a hundred, a most impressive sight, although their setting might have been more salubrious. Further into the hills, I had some splendid views of red kites, once common throughout most of the British Isles, but now restricted to this region of Wales. Seen against the sky as they soared above the moors, they were easily distinguishable from buzzards by their angled wings and forked tails, but against a dark background of trees or heather, it was the pale head and rich red body-colour that stood out.

That was in August, and the river was low after several weeks of fine weather. One morning I was fishing on the stretch below the town. I had not seen any sign of salmon and was concentrating on trout, fishing wet with a cast of 3 pounds breaking strain and a very small Peter Ross. As I fished slowly down the pool, I heard a splash behind me, and looking round, I thought for a moment that some unseen angler on the far bank (which was high and steep and covered with trees and bushes) was hauling a fish towards him across

An idyllic English scene: the River Lugg at Mordiford in Herefordshire.

the pool. Something long and grey with its head out of the water was moving fast across the still water on the near side of the pool. Then I realized that it was a grey squirrel. When it reached the middle of the pool, it got caught by a fast current and was drawn downstream towards the rough water below the pool tail, but it managed to claw its way in towards the far bank, and just as I thought it was about to be swept down the rapids, it reared up out of the water, caught hold of a branch of oak that hung low over the water, and swung itself up to safety. It shook the water from its coat, and scampered along the branch, quickly vanishing among the foliage.

I fished on, and presently Ray came walking across the meadow towards me, his lanner falcon on his fist. We had arranged to meet and lunch together at a pub, and I told him that I only needed a few more casts to cover the shallow glide at the tail of the pool. At almost the last cast I felt a steady, firm pull on the line, and thought for a second or two that I had snagged a branch under the water. Then my reel screeched, and something very large and very angry tore off downstream, through the rapids and into the pool below. Trees just below me prevented me from gaining the bank and running after it, and I had to stand there, helpless, as first the line and then the backing were stripped from the reel. The fish seemed bent on going straight back to Cardigan Bay and when nearly all the backing was gone, I was forced to apply pressure. A long way downriver the fish jumped, a splendid salmon that couldn't have been less than 15 pounds. The cast, of course, snapped, and as I sadly reeled in, the fish jumped again, landing with a mighty splash as if to impress upon me its extreme annoyance. If only, I thought to myself, I had persisted in fishing for salmon, instead of changing to my trout rod. But if I had done so, I would probably have been using a larger fly as well as thicker gut – certainly I would not have thought of using that tiny Peter Ross – and in the clear, shallow water of the pool-tail the salmon would, as likely as not, have remained aloof.

In the evenings, during that visit and a subsequent one in September, I fished for sea-trout and had some sport, though without encountering one of the very large sewin for which the Welsh rivers are famous. One evening, in the bar of the hotel where we were staying, I was introduced to a local expert, Dai, who promised to take me fishing that night, and show me where the big sewin lay and how to catch them. After quite a number of pints and a lot of fishing talk he went

Left. *Keeping a low profile: the River Teifi above Llanybydder in April, when the first salmon may be expected.*

Below. *Tawny owl hunting in the early evening.*

off to have his supper and I mine, having agreed to meet at ten o'clock. He kept coming back, shaking my hand very earnestly and saying, 'Ten o'clock, right? I'll be there; see you later, boyo,' but eventually he went, and having had my meal, I returned to the bar, dressed for the river. 'Going fishing again?' asked a large and jolly man who was perched on one of the bar stools. 'Yes,' I replied. 'Dai's coming to fetch me.' 'Oh, Dai's coming back, is he? H'm!' Ten o'clock came and went, and by eleven there was still no sign of Dai. 'It's odd,' I said, 'he seemed so very keen.' 'Yes,' answered my friend. 'Dai's keen, very keen indeed until he's had his tea, but then he goes to sleep and nothing in the world will wake him – but he's keen as mustard, is Dai, and he knows how to catch those big sewin.' I expect he did. As for me, I took off my waders and resigned myself to the fact that the sewin would have to wait for another day.

More recently, I visited the Teifi in late April, during a spell of exceptionally hot weather, but the salmon run had barely started and I had to content myself with catching a few trout on the dry fly. The secretary of the local club, whom I met on the river bank, told me that brown trout numbers had diminished in recent years, and blamed acid rain.

Another river with which I had a brief encounter was the Darent in Kent, a river once famed for its wild brown trout, but which suffered from the effects of pollution early in the century. The fish I caught were rainbow, obviously stocked fish, though I believe I am right in saying that the Darent is one of the few rivers in Britain where rainbows breed. My drawing of a tawny owl was prompted by an incident during that visit, when I was fishing in the golden light of dusk with long shadows creeping across the fields. I was in the shade of some alders, and must have been standing very still, for a tawny owl glided low overhead and dropped into the meadow grass only a few yards from me, where it pounced on a beetle or some other small prey. No doubt it had a hungry brood to feed, for tawnies are normally the most nocturnal of the owls. For the fisherman, hunting barn owls, until they became so scarce, were a much commoner sight.

Finally to Derbyshire, and the lovely, clear streams that wind through the dales. My first visit to the region, when I had arranged a week's fishing on the Wye, was spoilt by an accident. On the evening of my arrival a lorry had hit a tank of creosote on a road running by the river, and by next morning all the fish in the rivers downstream of the spillage were either dead or dying. To walk beside the river, and see hordes of dead fish – some of them well into the 2-pound class – floating downstream or bobbing in the slacks and backwaters, was a doleful sight indeed. I managed to get a day or two on the Dove, but the fish were considerably smaller and not very numerous, and for most of the week I consoled myself, instead, by exploring the dales and hunting for wildflowers, of which the region has a rich variety.

Recently I was in the area again. My fishing was on a part of the River Dove that runs through low-lying pastureland, and a strong downstream wind made casting a dry fly quite a challenging occupation. But I had some sport with both trout and grayling and also enjoyed several long walks beside the river in its higher reaches, where it runs through Dove Dale and Mill Dale. The steep-sided valleys, limestone rocks and stone walls and bridges give the area a marked individuality, and it was pleasant to muse, as we sauntered at the water's edge and my friend Alan turned up rocks to expose crayfish and miller's thumbs, that our feet must often have been standing, as it were, in the very footprints of Izaak Walton, and his co-author Charles Cotton whose house, Beresford Hall, once stood a little further upriver, in or near Beresford Dale. There were many places where one could imagine that the scene had changed very little in the intervening three-and-a-half centuries.

The River Dove, Mill Dale, in September.

A West Highland Spate River

All the way up the fissured and fragmented west coast of the Scottish Highlands, innumerable small rivers flow down from the mountains towards the sea. All of them hold brown trout, generally of very meagre proportions, and most of them attract runs of migratory fish – salmon and sea-trout – which each year battle their way up through rapids and over weirs and waterfalls and all manner of obstacles in search of ancestral spawning redds in remote glens or in tiny moorland burns. These are spate rivers, so called because they are fed by 'spates' or sudden floods caused by heavy rainfall. They rise and fall very rapidly and the fisherman must take every advantage of the brief periods when they are in prime condition, for during intervals of low water the job of coaxing a salmon or sea-trout from their attenuated runs and shrunken pools is a hard one. Their relatively small size and the dramatic fluctuations in water level mean that catches of fish are generally both smaller and more unpredictable than those of the larger and statelier rivers that flow eastwards towards the North Sea. But this only means that success, when it comes about, is all the more pleasurable, and, for the naturalists or anyone who loves the wild scenery of the western Highlands, these waters have other, compelling attractions.

One such river, that I know well, is the Moidart, which flows into the sea opposite the southern tip of the island of Skye via a tidal estuary in the form of a sea-loch some 3 miles in length and about a ½-mile across at its widest point. It has its source far up a mountain glen that is served only by a narrow pedestrian track, and is augmented in its gradual descent by the waters of numerous diminutive burns and by a cascade that flows down the mountainside from another small river in a higher valley. Two miles from the estuary it widens into a small loch, fringed with reeds and beds of white waterlilies, before plunging down a narrow gorge in a froth of white water. From this point to the road bridge at the head of the sea-loch, its stony streams and deep pools offer variable opportunities to the fisherman, according to the state of the water and the supply of fish in the estuary.

Each year, on arrival (generally in late June or early July), our first thought is to walk up on to the old single-span stone bridge – now superseded by a modern road bridge – and gaze down at the river below, noting the height of the water and peering into its amber depths in an effort to discern the dark shapes of fish, motionless in their traditional lies where rocks, or the set of the current, provide havens of slack water. They are hard to pick out, for the drab colouring of their backs is designed to blend perfectly with the boulders and pebbles beneath them, but when one is familiar with the lies, and if the reflections on the water's surface are not too bright, it may be possible to make out perhaps a small shoal of finnock or a couple of salmon. They rest there, just out of reach of the tide, accustoming themselves to the sensation of being once again in fresh water, before starting their journey upriver. By and by they will make their next move, often stopping a few

Fish-spotting from the old bridge over the River Moidart.

hundred yards upstream in the Nursery Pool, which is the principal holding pool of the river.

Last year the first evening's reconnaissance revealed a river reduced to a languid trickle, and no fish under the bridge beyond a few inconsiderable brownies. The next morning I walked right up the glen, to the loch and beyond, examining all the pools and lies as I went. There was hardly enough water coming down the river to fill a modest mountain burn; rocks and boulders stood high and dry and pebble banks which normally glittered golden under a foot or two of water now lay bleached and exposed in the sunlight. Even the Nursery Pool seemed as still and stagnant as a farmyard pond, reflecting the dark forest on the opposite bank like a mirror. But I was not too dispirited; a fortnight lay ahead of us, plenty of time for rain and spates, and in the mean time how could I complain as I walked the narrow road between hay meadows bright with wild flowers, the wayside banks rampant with bracken and foxgloves, the ditches full of yellow flag iris and pink-flowered valerian? Across a pasture where newly shorn ewes and well-grown lambs were grazing, I could see, picking their way through tall sedges at the wood's edge, three red deer hinds and a single calf, and above the woodland, half-way up the mountainside, a pair of buzzards floated on outstretched wings. Their mewing cries came to me clearly through the thin summer air. Further up the glen, where the flat, marshy meadows beside the river gave way to stony hill pastures, a heathland type of flora began to prevail: the tiny white flowers of heath bedstraw, yellow stars of tormentil and heath-spotted orchids with their frilly white or pink-spotted petals like milkmaids' frocks, ling and bell-heather – the latter just starting to flower – purple-blue milkwort, buttercups and eyebright. Near the river I found some purple spikes of northern marsh orchid and on its banks a single clump of globeflower with its large, globular, butter-yellow flower heads – a true montane species and unexpected so low down. Where, along the lower reaches of the river, the bird song had been provided by chiffchaffs and willow warblers, blackbirds and robins, now there were the tinkling notes of meadow pipits and the scolding calls of whinchats. But the most numerous birds were wheatears; adults and newly fledged young, as bold as house sparrows, they were my companions all the way up the glen, past the loch and over the steep pass into the next valley.

Oh, the limpid, pure air of these remote, high places, refreshing alike to mind and body! Why, one wonders, does anyone endure the polluted atmosphere, the constant cacophony and all the pressures and annoyances of urban life? The silence seems so absolute, so pervasive, that it takes time and concentration to realize that it is in fact made up of tiny sounds, some near at hand, some distant, but all imbued with a bell-like clarity: the sigh of a breeze through the heather, an insect buzzing, the far-off bleats of sheep, the lap of wavelets on the stony shore of a lochan – lovely, heart-uplifting sounds.

One sound generally associated with such places, but absent on this occasion, was the gurgle of water running through hidden channels in the peat. Even the largest of the mountain burns could show only a thin trickle, and all the lesser streams and water courses had dwindled to nothing. I could crumble the peat in my hand, it was so dry, and walk nearly dry-shod over mounds of sphagnum moss that would normally be as full of water as a wet sponge. I had come up from East Anglia where it had rained almost every day for the past month and it seemed paradoxical that here in the western Highlands, there should have been virtually no rain – and certainly no spates – over the same period and longer. However, as I turned to retrace my steps, there were signs that conditions might be changing. The sun shone from a clear sky, still, along the coast, but behind me, over the mountains, grey clouds were gathering and settling, and some of the higher tops were already hidden from view.

In fact, during the week that followed, this pattern was to repeat itself most days: dark clouds often hung low and

The Rock Pool in drought conditions.

menacing over the mountains, but although they looked pregnant with rain, they seemed unwilling to release it, and the most we got was the odd brief shower and sometimes an hour or two of thin drizzle.

I am not a great believer in fishing spate rivers for salmon in conditions of dead low water – there are always trout lochs in the neighbourhood which can be fished with a greater chance of success and tidal estuaries may prove profitable if sea-trout are in the offing; furthermore I find it depressing to have to fish pools as if they were still ponds, when even the head streams provide hardly enough current to swing the fly round, and when weed, rock and ever-hungry parr are likely to be all that is hooked. Having said that, I freely admit that an assiduous fisherman will sometimes catch a fish in even the most unpromising conditions – very, very seldom, I should imagine, in the heat of the day, but occasionally at dusk or in the misty half-light of dawn. To emphasize this point, I may mention that two of my friends, fishing the same river in the previous year when I was not present, did achieve singular successes in just such low-water conditions. They were fishing at night for sea-trout, and the streamy runs having produced no takes, Alastair had come down to the Nursery Pool, which is deep even at low water, and had exchanged his floating line for a sinker. He was using a 10 foot 6 inch rod and his fly was a small Silver Doctor. He fished carefully down the pool, where there was just enough flow to bring the fly round slowly in a wide arc, and near the tail of the pool, soon after midnight, he hooked and subsequently landed a 12-pound salmon. A couple of days later, John, who was due to leave for home that evening, decided to have an hour or two's fishing before starting on the long night journey. At one o'clock in the morning, also in the Nursery Pool, he hooked on a large Medicine, and landed, a nice fresh-run grilse of 6 pounds – his first salmon. Two salmon in three days caught on the fly between midnight and one o'clock in low-water conditions!

But to return to the current year, on Monday evening (we had arrived on Sunday when no fishing is allowed) Charlie and I decided to fish, just because it was the first evening and because one's enthusiasm at the start of a fishing holiday is always too great to allow one to sit idle indoors, however unpropitious the conditions. This is a river which used to have a considerable reputation for large runs of often heavy sea-trout – the record, a plaster cast of which is on a wall in the big house, was a monster of 19½ pounds – and although the sea-trout runs have now diminished in favour of salmon, we had hopes, albeit slender, of catching at least the odd finnock. In this we failed. The fly would hardly fish, so painfully weak was the flow of water, no fish showed (the certain knowledge of fish being present, however uncatchable, is always a morale-booster), and, to cap it all, it was one of those nights when the midges were out in their myriads. Insect repellent was totally ineffective against the onslaught and to get through the motions of casting, fishing and retrieving line without having to break off and desperately swipe at one's face and neck, was virtually impossible. If there had been any fish about, I believe that I was fishing so badly, in such a jerky and uncoordinated manner, that I had no chance of catching one. As it was, I fished – or went through the motions of fishing – for about an hour and a half, and then beat a disorderly retreat to my car, pursued by a cloud of midges. Charlie, who is made of sterner stuff, continued for several hours more, but with no greater success.

On Tuesday the showers were heavier and rather more frequent, and although none of the mountain burns had appreciably swelled in volume, some water must have been coming off the hills, for by Wednesday the river had risen a couple of inches – not much, but enough to liven it up considerably. At least a fly could now be given some semblance of life in the stronger currents and even the smallest freshet may, briefly and unpredictably, turn a 'potted' fish into a taker. So I fished again that evening, first at the Rock Pool, then at the Upper Nursery and finally, as the

*A meadow pipit in typical song flight: descending at a steep angle
with wings raised, tail spread and legs trailing.*

long northern twilight faded, beween half past eleven and midnight, into near darkness, at the Nursery. There were few midges about, and it was a magical night: warm, still, faintly luminous even after the last dull glow had melted away above the western horizon. I could no longer see my line as it hit the water, but somehow I managed to avoid catching the fly in the alder boughs that hung low over the water from the opposite bank. I was wading down the stream that leads into the pool, and below me Robin was fishing the pool itself. I could just make him out, a shadowy figure on the bank near the fishing hut, and at intervals I would hear the swish of his line as he made his cast. Two fish were rising periodically near the head of the pool, one of them at times only a few yards from me, another down towards the pool tail. The great, reverberating 'splosh' when a fish jumps in the stillness of the night never fails to make the heart beat faster. They are there, you think to yourself, only yards away; at the next cast one of them might – just might – be tempted to lunge at my fly! So one casts as carefully as possible, judging the length of line so as to cover the water without catching anything on the opposite bank, sensing the movement of the fly as it swings round across the current, always anticipating the moment when a tug on the line will indicate that a fish has taken. But this was not to be the night. I stopped fishing when the water became too deep to wade, and letting my line stream out in front of me, took out my pipe and lit it. From the wooded hillside to my left a tawny owl hooted; then a sandpiper flew upstream over my head, uttering its shrill, piping calls, and at almost the same moment, from somewhere beyond the pool tail, there came a great sound of splashing. For a moment I thought that Robin had hooked and was playing a fish, but then I realized that it was a herd of deer that had entered the shallows below the pool to drink. Their din lasted for five minutes or more, then they were gone and the night was given over once more to silence. I reeled up, and giving the fish best, presently joined Robin by the fishing hut. A dram apiece from his flask and

five minutes of desultory chat as we stood contemplating the black water of the pool, then we were off to our beds. An unproductive evening, but certainly not a wasted one.

Heath spotted orchids, bog asphodel and a wood tiger moth.

56

Up to the Hill Lochs

The next day I forsook the river and, accompanied only by my young labrador, set out to explore the hill lochs immediately to the north of the river's outflow. I took a trout rod with me, but my intention was rather to walk and to identify and reconnoitre some of the lochs than to spend all my time fishing. The lochs lie at a height of about 1,300 feet, and the ascent is steep, by way of a zigzag track that is taxing on flabby muscles accustomed to gentle Suffolk gradients. But it is a very rewarding climb, full of interest to the naturalist and presenting a succession of ever more spectacular views. And these hills are green, bright with flowers and friendly by comparison with the arid screes and grim wastes of eroded peat in north-west Sutherland, where I had been fishing the previous summer.

I started off through tall bracken, following the course of a dried-up burn until it met the track. The sun had come out and it was suddenly very hot; there was the scent of bog myrtle crushed underfoot and bush crickets were chirping away in the undergrowth. A persistent group of house flies attached themselves to me and buzzed annoyingly about my head, and blood-sucking horse flies were on the prowl as well. But the track climbed up now through birch and bracken woodland, and the dappled sunlight brought out hordes of dark green fritillaries and another, smaller fritillary which I never managed to approach close enough to identify with certainty. A wood warbler fluttered from tree to tree ahead of me, uttering its monotonous triple notes unceasingly as it hunted for insects among the birch leaves. Beside the track were heath-spotted and fragrant orchids in abundance, and an occasional butterfly orchid, and there were ferns, liverworts and mosses in the wet gullies, which intrigued me but which I did not have time to stop and examine. Half-grown froglets hopped aside at my approach and once a young roebuck appeared on the track above me and watched me briefly with ears pricked and black nose a-twitch before trotting off into the bracken. He kept turning back to look at me and even when he was over a hundred yards away I could see his large ears and upright, spiky horns, as he stared at me over the green bracken fronds. Then Islay came racing up the track behind me, and in a few graceful bounds he was gone.

The woodland came to an end at about 600 feet, and then it was grey rocks and heather and a myriad tiny flowers: tormentil and bedstraw, orchids and thyme, asphodel and cat's ear and the silky white banners of cotton sedge. And breathtaking views – immediately below, the big house, with its tall chimneys and steepled towers, reduced to the size of a child's toy, surrounded by its wooded policies and parkland full of grazing cattle and sheep; the beige sands of the estuary through which the river and its tributary creeks wound in great loops like a tattered silver ribbon; distant islands floating in a milky haze between sea and sky; and hills, dark green close to, then purple and grey, fading, like a series of fragile glass cut-outs, to the most ethereal of blues. Glints of white showed where lochs lay among the hills and over all the sky arched so immense that it was able to comprise several different weather systems. Over the sea it was pale cobalt blue, diluting downwards through aquamarine to pearly white near the horizon, with wisps of high cirrus and bars of darker cloud over the island of Skye. Above me banks, towers and citadels of cumulus, with their attendant outriders, sent dark, ever-changing shadows racing across the mountains, and eastwards, over the higher peaks, great masses of slate-grey nimbus hung low and a rainbow shimmered faintly at the head of the glen.

Still the track went up and up, turning inland now and weaving its way between bluffs of rock, slopes which were a patchwork of heather and tall grasses, and outcrops of pale grey, lichened rocks. It was cooler, now that we were well above the wood, but my little bodyguard of flies was still in attendance and I was grateful to a large golden-ringed dragonfly which suddenly zoomed into their midst, effectively dispersing them. The way was undulating, and as I arrived at each successive eminence, I expected to see the loch laid out before me. That last ½-mile seemed to continue for ever, but at last I topped a small hillock and there it was, its silver-grey surface criss-crossed by ripples, its coves and inlets divided by rocky spurs, and its little islands dark with pine trees. In bays protected from the wind the water was glassy calm, reflecting sky and clouds, every green spike of horsetail in the shallows faithfully mirrored. The silence was like a presence, and caused a ringing in my ears. I stood still and let it flow around and through me. Then it was broken by the loud cries of a common gull swooping low over the water. I could see a small flotilla of young gulls far out on the loch, and I imagine that numbers of them breed around its shores. We went down to the boathouse where I tackled up, ate a sandwich and smoked my pipe, while Islay played excitedly along the edge of the loch, in and out of the water. In the boathouse was a modern fibre-glass boat, somewhat patched and dented, and the rotting skeleton of a large old wooden boat. I was told that it had taken seven men to haul the fibre-glass boat up the track to the loch, but that the wooden boat, which must have

been considerably heavier, had been brought up by just two – mighty fellows they must have been.

For an hour or two I fished along the shore of the loch, between the rocky promontories and the small islets. The rocks shelved rapidly into deep water, and as no fish were rising, I fished a sinking line with a Greenwell's Glory on the point and a Black Pennell on the dropper. For years now I have used a very small selection of flies for all loch and lake fishing, changing the size but very seldom the pattern. Nymphs and dry flies apart, I have stuck to a Greenwell, or occasionally a Peter Ross, as the tail fly, with a Black Pennell or Zulu, if anything, on the bob. If fish are in a taking mood I believe that they will take these well-tried patterns as readily as any others and if they are not, as was the case this afternoon, then I very much doubt if any other combination of colours or materials would effect a radical change of mood. I have had sufficient success with my chosen patterns, over the years, to feel confidence in them, and that is half the battle. And when I have been fishing in company with other fishermen, I have never noticed that their different patterns have attracted more fish, although of course more skilful fishing and better tactics have often done so.

As it was, I caught just one small brown trout which went quickly back into the water, before packing up and setting off to explore some of the other lochs nearby. I followed the course of a little burn up a marshy valley dotted all over with the white tufts of cotton sedge, but kept to the higher slopes to one side, where the going was less squelchy. On the way I encountered a wood tiger moth, several large heath butterflies and the 2-inch long, hairy brown caterpillar of an oak eggar moth; I found two kinds of sundews – those curious bristly leaved carnivorous plants – and the pale green leaf rosettes of butterwort, each supporting a single stem and handsome

View over the Moidart estuary from the track that leads up to the hill lochs.

purple flower. Islay surprised a family of grouse – two adults and six or seven chicks just able to fly. She gave chase, and they flew 50 yards or so before settling again in the heather, but when I called her to heel one of the parent birds flew back and swooped at her in a brave display of aggression.

The burn led me to Lochan Meall a Mhadaich Mor, a high, lonely oblong of pewter-coloured water, whose surrounding hills plunged steeply down, suggesting awesome depths. No birds were on it, no fish rose, only the endless lines of ripples moved across its surface in their relentless advance and lapped, soundlessly, against its rocky shore. Inscrutable, it reflected the sky but gave no hint of what lurked in its dark, cold deeps. As I cast out my line and watched it slowly sink, I imagined the walls of rock descending further and further into an abyssal darkness more profound than any night, to a jumble of boulders on its bed that lay just where they had lain since the last glaciers retreated, ten thousand years ago or more. The thought sent a shiver down my spine, and I turned my attention to the upper layers of water, warmed by the sun, where I knew that there were trout – not many but large, 2 pounds and upwards, I had been told. None showed that day, and there was not so much as a nibble at my flies. The following week several of us came up to the lochs, and on that occasion we did see fish rise, and good fish too, though a ½-pounder from the first loch was the only catch. We tried sinking lines and floaters, wet flies and nymphs, large flies and small, but the big fish were indifferent to all that we could offer them.

Before turning towards home, I went on to one other lochan, smaller and surrounded by even steeper slopes. From a hill-top overlooking it there was a splendid view, commanding the whole peninsula and out over the sea to the islands of Rhum and Eigg and beyond them to the misty blue hills of

Loch nan Paitean, high in the Moidart hills: a fine place for the fisherman who enjoys solitude.

Skye. I fished this little loch also, for half an hour or so, and then, as the sky began to flush with the warm tints of evening, made my way back to the boathouse and wearily down the mountainside, spurred on by the thought of a large whisky before dinner.

On the Saturday it rained steadily all morning, but cleared and brightened in the afternoon. Charlie, Robin and I took a boat out on Loch Shiel, a long, narrow loch over 17 miles in length, joined to the sea by a short but beautiful and prolific river. The part of the loch we were fishing lies between flat 'mosses' or marshy grasslands which extend into the loch from both sides in the form of shallow sandbanks, the channel of deep water between them varying from 100 yards or so to ¼ mile. We tried to arrange our drifts so as to keep close to the edges of the sandbanks, for this is where the shoals of sea-trout congregate, and before very long Robin and Charlie had each caught a finnock of about ¾ pound. Soon after, as we were negotiating 'the Narrows', where opposing sandbanks approach each other very closely, I hooked a fish of similar size but quickly lost it. At the time we had the engine puttering away very slowly, as we were manœuvring into position for the next drift. Once the fish was lost the engine was re-started and we turned back over the spot where I had hooked it. I re-cast and almost immediately was into a much larger fish. I only glimpsed it briefly as it boiled at the fly, for after that it first took out line then came back fast and deep under the boat and never showed again. It was certainly over 3 pounds, but how much over I was not destined to discover, for after playing it for about five minutes, the line went slack, and I experienced that empty feeling of disappointment with which all fishermen are familiar. The fact that both fish were hooked while the outboard motor was running probably contributed to their loss. The extra speed of the fly through the water means that the fish does not have time to turn with it, so that it gets hooked in the front of the mouth rather than securely in the scissors – a good reason for fishing the drift

61

properly, despite the need for constant casting and fast retrieval, rather than succumbing to the temptation of lazily trolling the fly.

Meanwhile, the morning's steady rain, though it had hardly caused the river to rise, had livened it up and that evening the son of the river's proprietor, fishing the stream into the Dam Pool, caught a 6-pound grilse. We had been put upon our mettle, but another Sunday lay ahead before we could again try our luck on the river.

Dark green fritillaries.

Opposite. *Grilse fresh from the sea.*

A Spate at Last

It rained again on Saturday, and on Sunday, at long last, we had a whole day of continuous, heavy rain. I spent most of the day indoors, reading beside the log fire or tying flies, and watching with satisfaction as the mountainsides, below their pall of low-lying cloud, became streaked with threads and tassels of white which gradually increased in size throughout the day. By late afternoon, as I stood by an open window, the roar of all these rushing waters drowned out the softer drumming of the rain. There was that delicious, earthy, fungal smell that heavy rain distils from rank vegetation and sometimes, mixed with it, the aromatic scent of wood smoke borne down in eddies from the chimney.

The rain eased off towards evening and finally stopped. From the dinner table, instead of making for armchairs by the fire, we were all drawn, as by a magnet, towards the river. And what a transformation had taken place: under the old bridge the water came through in a jostling, turbulent, foaming torrent, the colour of dark sherry. Such a surge of

fresh water, I thought, must surely set every salmon and sea-trout fin a-quiver, from the bridge to the open sea.

We walked on up to the Nursery Pool through a dark and dripping alleyway of rhododendrons and vast and ancient cypress trees. Between their corrugated boles and ponderous, downcurving branches like the trunks of mastodons, we could glimpse the river as it tore along, its leaping wavelets golden in the sunset light. At the Nursery Pool we found the water lapping at the base of the fishing hut and sheets of floodwater were spreading across the adjoining meadow, fed by the powerful gush of water from a culvert. The pool itself was a black and seething cauldron, with swirling eddies swallowing themselves up in spiralling vortices and huge eruptions convulsing its surface. The stream at its head had become a smooth, swift, golden-brown glide that broke up into contending currents, foam and angry, choppy waves as it entered the pool, and creamed hungrily around the submerged boles of alder trees at its edges. Up and down the glen the only sounds that could be heard were the sounds of water – water thundering over the falls, cascading down the mountainsides, gurgling in the ditches and culverts, water leaping and crashing through boulder-strewn rapids and swishing down the level runs, water dripping from the branches of trees.

By six o'clock the next morning we were on the river, and a lovely, clear, rain-washed morning it was, the air so rarefied that every detail of the surrounding landscape, to the furthest hills, was sharp, the colours bold and undiluted. Walking down to the river the grass was all a-sparkle with drops of moisture, and sooty black chimney sweeper moths rose and fluttered away at my approach. The water level had fallen during the night and the river, though still high, flowed more calmly now. I started my operations in the stream that runs into the Dam Pool, to the accompaniment of anxious calls from a sandpiper that probably had young in the vicinity, and

The Nursery Pool on the morning after a spate.

flew back and forth above my head in an agitated manner. I fished with eager anticipation, for conditions were as perfect as they would ever be and every ripple on the water's surface spoke of salmon ready and keen to take my fly. But by the time my line was swinging round in a broad, slow arc towards the falls at the lower end of the Dam Pool, my spirits were a trifle dampened, for the sun was rising and no fish had stirred. After taking a look at the tricky currents and violent undertows in the Rock Pool, I decided to give it a miss and went on down to the Nursery, where I found John, who had already fished down the run into the head of the pool and was now fishing the pool itself. Fish were rising and, with hope renewed, I started fishing well back up the run.

Meanwhile, upriver, Charlie had fished down from the March Pool and had reached a part of the river known as the Cailleach or Old Woman. It is hardly a pool, though it has some pool-like attributes, its main features being a series of deep pots under the near bank, divided by large rocks, the bed of the stream shelving down from shallows on the far side. Upstream a line of large boulders crosses the river at an oblique angle, creating a kind of natural weir. The pots are not fishable from the near bank, and Charlie decided to make the somewhat perilous crossing by way of the weir – the river still running high and strong – in order to fish into the pots from the far side. It was a good strategy, for very soon he was into a salmon, but getting it across the fierce current in order to land it in the shallows was less easy. Perhaps he was impatient and hauled too hard, perhaps it was just insecurely hooked; in any event, after ten minutes, with his net out and ready, he and the fish parted company. Losing a fish is always a sad business, but in this case it was especially so because no one had caught a fish from the Cailleach in recent memory.

Back at the Nursery, feeble ghosts of the previous night's great whirlpools formed ever-changing arabesques on the surface of the water, and flecks of foam, in endless fleets, sailed into the pool and were whirled around in a mad dance

66

before being despatched down the river. The sun was well up by now and the shingle bank where I was wading glowed like fire-amber through the peat-stained water. The bank sloped down towards a deep channel against the far bank, where a strong current ran. About half-way along this channel was a large humped boulder, invisible now but well known to us as providing a favourite lie. The moment my Silver Stoat's-tail passed beyond this boulder, it was taken. I was into a salmon at last – and a most peculiar fish it proved to be. I may as well confess straight away that it was a small, though fresh-run, grilse, weighing just 5 pounds but that it took me an inordinately long time to land. During all that time it never moved more than 3 yards from where it was hooked, and for a long time never came near the surface. It just bored down and, sticking its nose into the pebble bed of the stream, refused to budge. I was using a 10-foot carbon fibre trout rod and a cast of 7 pounds breaking strain, and gave it all the stick I dared, but each time I managed to force it towards the shallows it gave a powerful wriggle and returned to its station out of sight at the bottom of the deep channel. I couldn't persuade it to run upstream – or indeed to run anywhere – and I couldn't get below it since the water quickly became too deep to wade and trees at the water's edge prevented me from proceeding along the bank. At long last it weakened and Charlie, who had come down from the Cailleach, netted it out for me. Both he, and John, who had been watching the whole proceedings with an increasingly jaundiced eye, declared it to be the most boring fish (in more senses than one) that they had ever seen. It was the smallest salmon I have caught, yet took me longer to land than any other. A similar-sized fish, this year, was netted in little over five minutes. My fish's back was covered with long-tailed sea-lice and it ate most deliciously next evening.

That was the last spate we had and the rest of the week was divided between fishing the declining waters of the river, the estuary where we caught a few small finnock or sea-trout smolts but nothing keepable, the hill lochs and Loch Shiel. My most enjoyable day was the last when, in the afternoon, Mike and I took a boat out on Loch Shiel. I caught two good, fighting finnock, an ounce either side of 1 pound, the second and larger of which indulged in five spectacular leaps, high out of the water, flashing like a bar of silver in the sunlight, before being brought to the net. I also caught two smaller fish which hooked themselves almost simultaneously, the one on the bob, the other on the tail fly. Mike dexterously managed to scoop them both together into the net, but as they were under ¾ pound, I released them. It was a lovely, placid afternoon, with only a light ripple on the water. As we came back in the evening the hills to the west were silhouetted in the darkest imaginable green – the colour of a pool in a pine forest – with a corona of light along their crests, and as the breeze died away they were mirrored in the glassy calm waters of the loch. A red-throated diver flew overhead and in front of us a red-breasted merganser made a glittering path through the water as she led a brood of no less than twenty youngsters out of our way. When we beached the boat they came in close to the shore and all started diving, the ducklings leaping out of the water like porpoises in order to give impetus to their dives. Sometimes the whole lot would disappear for a few seconds, only to come bobbing up to the surface like so many corks. How the mother bird had come to acquire such a large brood, I cannot imagine, for I can find no record of more than seventeen eggs for the species, seven to twelve being more usual. Mergansers are traditional enemies of the fisherman, and it is surprising how well they have survived, considering the persecution they have suffered over many years. As is so often the case where species are harried in the interest of game preservation, there is little justification, for trout and salmon form only a very small part of the merganser's diet.

Charlie playing a salmon at the Cailleach.

Sea-trout

I have yet to catch a big, or even a biggish sea-trout, my largest to date being just 3 pounds, and perhaps I never will unless I become more adept at the art of night fishing than I can presently claim to be. In large expanses of water the sea-trout can be caught as readily as any other fish during the daytime, but in the close confinement of a river they become extremely wary and, apart from small finnock (also variously known as whitling, herling or school-peel), are seldom caught except during the hours of darkness, especially the really big fish. Of course there are exceptions and when a river is carrying a heavy run of fish, particularly in falling water immediately after a spate, there is always the chance that an odd one will break the rules and get itself caught in broad daylight. I always think of Negley Farson's description in *Going Fishing* – perhaps the best fishing book of them all – of the 8- (possibly 10-) pounder that he played for a long time, and lost, while fishing a peaty burn in the Shetlands. And on the first occasion that I ever went fishing for sea-trout one of our party, a skilful angler, caught a 3½-pound sea-trout one morning on a dry fly while fishing for brown trout.

That was on the Kilkerran water of the River Girvan in Ayrshire, a long time ago, when I was very much of a novice in the use of a fly rod under any circumstances, let alone when wading a tree-girt river at dead of night. I remember the first night of that July holiday with an awful clarity. There were

Sandpiper below the Dam Pool, with the water still rising after a spate.

four or five of us in the party, and more of our friends were fishing on another estate, further upriver. We were all quite young, as we were at college at the time, but I was the only novice in the party, all the others having fly-fished since boyhood. I had fished the river all through the first day, and had studied the water that had been allotted to me for the first night session. It consisted of a streamy, boulder-strewn run leading down to a long, narrow pool. Much of the wading was fairly deep, and there were oaks, alders and bramble bushes growing from the banks, but it did not seem to present any great problems and I fished it down in the morning without mishap. It was left undisturbed during the afternoon and I did not see it again until after we had had dinner. We set out at about ten o'clock in the evening and, wishing each other 'tight lines', dispersed towards different sections of the river. I remember being full of excitement as I walked across a dewy meadow redolent of cow-dung where a herd of Ayrshires was grazing, and as I neared the river I could hear, above the babble of the water, the loud 'sploshes' of sea-trout. But when I reached the bank and looked down at the black, foam-flecked water racing by, it seemed rather forbidding and bore a decidedly less kindly aspect than it had done in the morning when the sunlight had glanced on its surface and lit the boulders on its bed. Gingerly, I lowered myself into the dark flood, and as I fumbled to release the tail fly from the rod ring and pull off a length of line, it occurred to me that the current had grown stronger, and the boulders very much bigger, than they had been in the morning. I was fishing, in my innocence,

with a team of three wet flies, probably some such selection as Butcher, Alexandra and Soldier Palmer, and from the very first cast I was in trouble. That was in the gloaming, and although the northern midsummer night never becomes pitch-dark, it was to get a lot darker yet.

I cannot now remember every detail of that disastrous night; suffice it to say that calamities came thick and fast. My flies hooked trees behind me and on the opposite bank, rocks in the river and, continuously, each other. The cast tied itself into birds' nests of appalling complexity, and I slipped on a slimy boulder, filling both waders with water and only narrowly avoiding total immersion. There was hardly a moment when my flies were actually fishing, and altogether it was a most dispiriting experience. Sometime during the night I did learn my first lesson and exchanged the ruined cast for a new one with a single fly on the point, but by that time it was very dark and my travails were only marginally reduced. During all these goings-on I was mocked by the constant, reverberating splashes of rising sea-trout, all of which, I need hardly say, remained in firm occupation of their natural element. At length I gave up the unequal struggle and walked up the river to find out how my companions were faring. They had had a marvellous night's fishing and all had caught fish.

Surprisingly enough I did finally catch my first sea-trout during that week. I had been charitably allotted the most open stretch of water on the beat, with the easiest wading. It probably also had the least potential for catching sea-trout, but at least it gave me a chance to practise judging the length and angle of my casts in the dark. I thought I was doing quite well, but then I noticed a familiar whistling sound as I made my cast, and quickly reaching up I found, as I had suspected, that the leader had once again developed a bird's nest. Cursing, I waded towards the bank and, by the light of a torch

Leaping sea-trout.

70

tucked under my arm, began to wrestle with the hideous thing. The more I worked at it, the worse it became, and I had almost decided to give up and mount a new cast when a tall figure loomed up beside me out of the darkness. It was not one of our party, but a local man, for I was on a part of the water where we did not have exclusive rights.

'Och,' he said, 'I see ye have a wee bit o' trouble,' and taking the rod from me, he examined the bird's nest and then, to my utter amazement, with a few deft pulls at the loops which emerged from the nucleus of the tangle, began to unravel it. In a matter of minutes we had the whole thing sorted out. He looked at my fly, which was a Bloody Butcher, and taking a round tobacco tin from his pocket, he said, 'Ye'll be wanting a couple o' these on y're flee.' With that he extracted two fat white maggots from the tin and impaled them on the end of the hook. 'Noo then,' he went on, 'ye'll do nae good whatever fishing here,' and beckoning me to follow, he led the way downriver until we came in sight of the tail of a large pool, where the water narrowed and rippled over a shallow bed of shingle before plunging down a rocky gradient bordered by trees. Putting a finger to his lips and indicating that I should wade with extreme caution, my guide showed me where to stand and where to aim my fly. After the first cast he told me to get out another couple of yards of line. 'But nae false casting,' he admonished. 'Just *lift* the line and *lay* it doon – that's right!' Following his instructions I moved forward several yards, until my fly was swimming round just at the end of the smooth glide before the start of the broken water. 'Noo . . . then,' I heard him say, as if he knew exactly what was going to happen, and the next second there was a splash on the water surface and a fierce tug on the line, and I was reeling in as hard as I could as the fish came belting up the pool. I don't remember the details of the fight, so I won't attempt to describe it, but five or ten minutes later I had my

Sea-trout fishing – almost time to start.

first sea-trout, a lovely silver fish of just over 2 pounds, on the bank. I shall always be grateful to that kindly man, who gave up an hour of his own fishing time to help a complete stranger. I certainly would have had to wait some time longer for my first sea-trout, without him.

Since then I have always welcomed any opportunity that has come along to fish for sea-trout at night, for it is a very exciting kind of fishing, but although my general technique has inevitably improved over the years, I have never become very adept at night-fishing, and I have to admit that I still catch trees at least as often as I catch fish. Perhaps this is because opportunities have been rather few and far between, but I have a suspicion that good night-fishers, like good Latinists, violinists or horsemen, are born, not made.

I caught my next two sea-trout a few years later, on the River Stinchar, the next river south from the Girvan, and then another on the River Torridge in Devonshire on a night that went on to become so impenetrably dark that I defy anyone to have been able to fish successfully; but my best night's fishing, which included the capture of the 3-pounder, was on a very small Argyllshire river, when I stopped at the local hotel, at the head of a big sea-loch, on my way up towards Cape Wrath. I had stayed at the same hotel as a small boy with my mother during the war, and had in fact caught my first-ever brown trout in the river. It was about 3 inches long and taken, I need hardly say, on a worm.

The River Goil is a very modest stream, little more than a hill burn for much of its length, but both grilse and sea-trout travel up it to spawn. I spent a long time, that July evening, strolling or sitting beside it as I waited for the light to fade before starting to fish, breathing in the crisp air, laced with the tang of salt, and spellbound by the almost overpowering magnificence of the mountain scenery all around me. I remember a pair of buzzard that flew mewing out of a forestry plantation a little way above me, and then went soaring upwards in great interweaving spirals until they were mere dots against the deepening ultramarine of the sky, and I watched a dipper as it repeatedly plunged into the torrent from a half-submerged rock in mid-stream. From the loch I could hear the cries of gulls and the faint piping calls of oystercatchers and other small waders as they flew along the tide-line, and from the hills inland came the long drawn-out bubbling trill of a curlew.

Gradually the mountains darkened until they were deep purple silhouettes and the river took on a coppery sheen with wine-dark reflections. For a long time after the sun had set, the western sky was flushed with dying embers of light, and when I started fishing there was still light enough to see where my flies fell and follow the snaking movements of my floating line. I caught two fish of about a pound each quite early on, and then after a long gap, when the last, smouldering traces of the sunset had vanished and the river was a molten stream of dull silver, my Dunkeld was taken quite softly as it completed its swim across the current at the tail of a small, rocky pool. So softly was it taken that it was only when I raised my rod tip to cast again that I realized the fish was there. But once the line tightened it was galvanized into action and soon I was stumbling among tussocks of sedge as I hurried downstream in an effort to keep abreast of it. It passed swiftly down some turbulent water among a clutter of rocks where I feared for my frail cast, and reaching another little pool, where the water divided and swirled around a large rock on which some tufts of heather and a birch sapling had taken root, it jumped three times in succession, great, cartwheeling leaps which set my heart pounding and sent glinting rings of silver radiating out across the black reflections in the water. The rest of battle was fought doggedly, and my only problem occurred when the fish retreated round the back of the big rock. The birch sapling prevented me from lifting my line over the top of it, and I had to wait some time for the fish to tire before I could work it back towards me and the waiting net. As I lifted it from the water, the hook came away from its mouth and I shuddered to think how nearly I had lost it. It weighed almost exactly 3 pounds.

Last summer I spent a week with hospitable friends on the Isle of Arran. We fished two small streams, the Iorsa Water and the Machrie Water which, though they run parallel to each other, only a few miles apart, are of quite different character. The Machrie descends in a series of rocky pools, first through dense birch and bracken woodland, and then through pasture-land, and carries a run of salmon as well as sea-trout. The Iorsa runs down a steep-sided valley between bare, green hills which rise to a height of about 1,500 feet. Some 2 miles above the sea it widens into a narrow loch – Loch Iorsa – and then continues at a steep gradient with very few pools except those that have been artificially created by means of large boulders placed across the stream. In spate the peat-stained water comes roaring down in a froth of white foam-caps, all the way to the sea. It appears to be almost exclusively a sea-trout water, although I did catch one fingerling brown trout in the brackish water of the estuary. The west coast of Arran is washed by the Gulf Stream, and has a mild climate. Fuchsia grows in the hedges, and on both the Iorsa and the Machrie the brilliant orange-scarlet flower-sprays of *Crocosmia*, growing luxuriantly at the water-side, lend an exotic note to the scene.

Both rivers were in full spate when I arrived, and the next morning I went out very early and fished the bottom beat of the Machrie above the road bridge, with the rain still teeming down, but the water not too coloured to be fishable. The nicest-looking pool was called the Optimist, where a salmon was head-and-tailing at regular intervals. I could not interest it in my Silver Stoat's-tail double, but I got a distinct pluck which I felt certain was a sea-trout pulling at the long hackle. To test my theory I exchanged my cast for a lighter one and tied on a size 8 Dunkeld. I was taken at the first cast and landed a 1-pound sea-trout. Later in the week, following a second spate, I fished below the bridge and, again in pouring rain, began to get the kind of short takes which suggested finnock. On went the sea-trout cast and Dunkeld once more and, in the Tidal Pool at high tide, I had some exhilarating sport for an hour or so, taking finnock from the shoal and playing them upstream. Five came to the net, but all were under the pound mark and were put back.

Returning to the cottage for a late breakfast, I stopped at the roadside where it ran along beside the sea shore, to watch the birdlife along the line of the ebbing tide. There were diving gannets, about thirty red-breasted mergansers, a heron, eiders, oystercatchers, curlew, razorbills, a pair of velvet scoters and a pair of red-throated divers. Among a group of gulls which included greater and lesser black-backed, black-headed, herring and common, I spotted a single kittiwake, a normally pelagic species which till then I had seen only on its breeding cliffs on Handa Island.

Most of the fish that had been caught on the Iorsa during the previous week had been small finnock, between ½ and ¾ pound, and my own efforts produced similar results. Our one attempt at a night session was a failure. This was at least in part due to the riverside terrain which was hard enough to negotiate in daytime but quite impossible in the dark. Where I was fishing, below the loch, it consisted of large, humpy tussocks of purple moor grass interspersed with clumps of rushes, bog myrtle and occasional tufts of bell-heather and ling. The whole area was intersected by innumerable hidden gullies and narrow channels and an unwary step plunged one thigh-deep into viscous peat. Further downriver tall bracken came down right to the river's edge; I know of no more infuriating plant to the fisherman, wrapping any loose line that it can reach about its sinewy stems and between its numerous tough fronds, so that I have often had to use a penknife on it to release my line. Bracken must have caused the loss of many a fish.

We were fishing after the second, mid-week spate, so the water was too high to wade, and progress along the bank in the dark was exceedingly slow. In any event I had by this time begun to suspect that the larger sea-trout did not tarry long in the rough waters of the river, but took advantage of a spate to run straight up to the loch. For some reason we could not have the use of the boat on Thursday, but on Friday, my last day, Stefa (my hostess) and I fished up the river in the morning, and in the afternoon took the boat out on the loch. The mist had been rising and falling over the hills, letting through occasional shafts of sunlight, but now it dispersed and the day became very warm, though with sufficient breeze to put a ripple on the water.

Driving up the glen we had been stopped by an eyass peregrine on the track, which stood its ground and glared at us before taking off and flying away low over the bracken. Now, at the boathouse, we saw two more peregrines on the soar. There were numerous dragonflies about, most of them common hawkers splendidly enamelled in shades of brown, green and sky blue, but also a single male black darter. We

An adder sunning itself on a rock in Loch Iorsa.

saw adders, too: one, right at my feet, was coiled up between two tussocks of molinia; another, after we were afloat, was sunning itself on a rock several yards out from the shore and remained perfectly immobile when we rowed up to take a closer look, only its poised head and glittering eye showing that it was intensely aware of our presence. As soon as we had moved on, it slipped into the water and disappeared. Beautiful and unaggressive creatures, adders inspire an atavistic dread and have been needlessly slaughtered throughout the ages. Now at last it seems possible that they may soon be given the protection of the law in Britain.

That, however, is to anticipate events. While I was tackling up, Stefa walked down to the edge of the loch close to where it narrowed into the river, and began casting. A few minutes later she gave a shout; looking up, I saw her rod nicely arched, and grabbing a landing net, I ran down to join her. I was just in time to see a fish of well over 2 pounds splash on the surface and then we both gasped as the rod straightened and the line went slack. She had done everything right and I could hardly believe such bad luck, but when we examined the fly, a Blue Zulu, we found that the gape had straightened out. She was quite sure that it had been all right when she tied it on a few minutes before, so it must have been a poor-quality hook.

We had taken the boat over from a party of three who had been fishing earlier in the afternoon and had not had any luck, but as we shoved off from the mooring we saw that there were plenty of fish rising – most of them just dimpling the surface – and before long, fishing a Mallard and Claret, I had caught two fish which at 1¾ and 1½ pounds were at least considerably better than any we had had from the river. We saw one large fish jump, probably 5 pounds or over. I do not know if any salmon run the Iorsa, but if they do this could well have been one, for it rose on the far side of the loch, where the water was shallow, a lie more typical of salmon than of sea-trout. We failed to rise it, but we had little doubt that this was where we ought to have been concentrating our efforts earlier. I wondered, also, about the more placid waters of the upper river, which were harder work to reach since the track ended at the boathouse, but which might well carry more sedentary stocks of fish than the rough and comfortless waters of the lower reach. Alas! fishing holidays are never long enough to find out all the answers, and the secrets of the upper Iorsa will have to remain hidden for the present.

Afloat on the Loch

To fish the larger lochs, particularly those which hold sea-trout and salmon as well as brown trout, usually requires the use of a boat, and where no special rules apply, the angler has the choice of two alternative methods, trolling and dapping, besides traditional wet-fly fishing.

My only experience of trolling was when I was staying with a friend, many years ago, in Wester Ross, and we spent the best part of a day on one of the blackest and most forbidding lochs that I have ever encountered, trolling spinning baits in the hope of attracting one of the huge ferox for which the loch was famed. It was early in the year and the weather was chill. Mean gusts of wind came funnelling down the ravines between the mountains that bordered the loch, whose sheer granite cliffs plunged vertiginously down into the dark water. Squalls of icy rain hammered at the surface of the water and creamed the spindrift from the crests of the waves; they seemed to drag the clouds down with them from the mountain tops, and as they followed each other up the loch it was as if veils of tattered gauze writhed and billowed on the wind. The scene would have been transformed for us, I am sure, if a great cannibal trout had taken one of our lures. As it was I made my stint at the oars last as long as possible, since sitting still was cold work, and longed for the moment when we could honourably retire.

As for dapping, which involves presenting a big, bushy fly in an attractive, dancing manner on and just above the surface of the water, by means of a long rod and a silken blow-line, it has the merit that the take, when it comes, is dramatic and exciting. There are times, too, when it may be more effective than wet-fly fishing, although there are other times when the opposite is true. I have had four sea-trout in a row fishing wet-fly, when the occupants of three or four other boats nearby, all of whom were dapping, had not a single offer. But my own preference for the traditional method of loch fishing stems purely from the fact that if I am fishing from a boat, I like to be doing something all the time; the action of casting and retrieving line keeps you busy, and prevents you from getting too cold. You feel that you are actively in charge of the situation, casting towards likely lies according to the depth of water and the configuration of rocks and banks beneath the surface, and varying the speed and rhythm of retrieval and the length of the casts as necessary. In dapping, by comparison, you have to sit immobile for long periods, subject to the vagaries of the wind, and action only comes when a fish is hooked.

I like to use a rod of at least 10 foot 6 inches for boat fishing, and a long cast with some well-tried pattern as tail fly, such as Peter Ross, Mallard and Claret, or Black Pennell. The bob fly is always something large and bushy, often a Black Zulu, which

Two loch-caught sea-trout and a brownie.

acts rather like a dap as the line is retrieved, dancing over the ripples and frequently attracting a fierce take at the last moment. I do not bother, these days, with a fly on the middle dropper: it does not seem to me greatly to increase one's chances of catching a fish, but it certainly increases the chances of getting in a tangle, particularly on a windy day.

In England natural lakes are few and far between, except in the Lake District. There are reservoirs, but these tend to be overcrowded for my taste, and frequent introduction of stock fish means that one is often catching fish which bear all the signs of being fresh from the stew-pond. The lochs of Scotland, on the other hand, are legion. For the angler who enjoys a combination of good fishing, splendid scenery and solitude, the choice is almost endless. To some people loch fishing is boring by comparison to river fishing; to me it is just a different experience, with its own special attractions.

I think of a warm, breezy day in early August, spent on Loch Assapol in the Ross of Mull, as typical of the more relaxed aspect of loch fishing. It produced no large fish, but all that were caught were eaten and enjoyed; they gave good sport, the weather was fine and the surroundings wild and beautiful – what more could one wish for? In the morning, accompanied only by my yellow labrador dog, Danny, who was a patient, if not very enthusiastic, partner on such excursions, I rowed slowly up the loch, exploring various little bays and inlets which seemed to offer the chance of a trout, but caught only a few tiddlers. At the head of the loch the water shallowed and beds of pondweed grew from the silt brought down by the feeder burn. Trout were dimpling the barely ripped surface of the water, and before long I had caught a fish of about 6 ounces. However, my flies kept hooking the long stems of weed and presently I moved on a little way, gently lowered the anchor, and changing my cast for a greased one with a dry fly attached, set to work again, casting to the rises. I missed a lot, but at the end of an hour had caught three more trout. To stretch my legs and give Danny a run, I pulled the boat up on the shore and had my lunch sitting among the heather, bog myrtle and clumps of dwarf willow beside the outfall of the little burn. Scotch argus butterflies fluttered up into the air as Danny galloped through the heather and I watched first a distant pair of buzzards on the soar, and then a hen harrier as it glided low over the moorland, quartering the ground in leisurely flight, occasionally giving a few wing-beats to maintain its momentum.

In the afternoon the breeze freshened, and since the trout had gone off the rise, I rowed clear of the weeds then drifted

Storm brewing over a Sutherland loch.

down the loch, fishing all the way, towards the southern shore, which was rockier than the shore that I had followed in the morning. Ignorant of the underwater topography, I had to take my chance as to where the fish might be, but as I approached the shore I felt a tug on my line, followed by a flash of silver as a finnock leapt clear of the water. I netted it after a short, sharp fight, cast again and soon hooked another. By the time I had brought this one also to the net, I was almost on the rocks, so I rowed back for several hundred yards, then drifted down again and was rewarded with a third fish. A further drift failed to locate the shoal, and I rowed back across the loch with thoughts of tea in mind. In the evening I took my host's young nephew, to whom I had been giving some casting instruction, up to the head of the loch, and saw him catch his first trout, a nice fish of nearly ¾ pound, which gave me as much pleasure as any of the fish I had caught myself. We caught several more smaller trout, and it was dusk by the time we left the weedy shallows and started for home. The breeze had dropped again, and there was hardly a ripple on the water now. I rowed slowly in the same direction that I had drifted earlier in the afternoon. My companion held one of the rods with the flies trolling on a long line in our wake, but we failed to rise any more fish except one fingerling trout. As we came near to the shore I looked behind me, anxious to avoid any submerged hazards, the boat being old and frail. Fifty yards down the shore I thought I saw a movement on the horizon where the rocks were silhouetted against the sunset glow in the sky. I stopped rowing and we drifted on almost parallel to the shore. Something shiny and sinuous was moving about on the flat top of a large, detached rock. I thought at first it was a bird, but then its head came up and the blunt muzzle and the strong, tall column of the neck told me that it was an otter. We sat very still and presently it turned its head towards us; as we drifted closer, I could see its whiskers and little rounded ears sharply etched against the luminous sky. One forepaw was resting on the fish that it had

79

been eating, and it watched us intently for several seconds before suddenly, in one undulating, graceful movement, it seemed to slide down the face of the rock and disappeared under the water with hardly a ripple. The remains of the fish were left behind.

Otters are proverbially wary creatures, as well they might be considering the persecution they have suffered at the hands of men over the centuries. Often one can fish, year after year, a river which they are known to frequent, and never see any sign of them beyond some tracks in the mud, a pile of spraints or at best a trail of bubbles in the water. Fishing at dusk, I have heard their fluty whistles, but only on one other occasion have I seen a wild otter, and that was not on loch or river, but on a wild and rocky sea shore. However, they can, on occasion, be surprisingly bold. Following the ebb tide out across the mudflats of Loch Moidart, last summer, at about half past four in the morning, my friend Charlie had splendid views of an otter playing by itself on the muddy banks of the main channel. It must have been well aware of his approach across the open flats, but did not submerge and swim away until he was within a matter of 20 yards of it. Soon after that a small herd of half a dozen red deer hinds crossed the estuary from one side to the other, tripping through the shallow waters of the receding tide and swimming across the broad

Otter alerted – Loch Assapol, Mull.

channel which carried the river water out to sea. Such sights make an early start worthwhile, even if one does return with an empty creel.

For every day that I have spent in a boat on a loch when it has been warm and pleasant as on that Assapol day, there have been many more when the wind has moaned and the rain has fallen in a deluge – the sort of weather that is more easily enjoyed if the fish are in a taking mood. I would not, myself, take a boat out on a large loch in a very strong wind. It is dangerous and disagreeable, and unlikely to be productive of fish. But in the Highlands, winds can blow up very suddenly and with hardly any warning, as happened to me once when I was fishing with a friend on Loch More in Sutherland. My companion was not a fisherman, but had come for the ride, and was willing to take control of the boat, while I fished. When we started off there were patches of blue in the sky, and all the mountain-tops were visible. The quartz screes on the flanks of Ben Screavie glistened and when the sun broke through the clouds, the mosaic of boulders on the low hills beside the loch shone white as bleached bones, against their background of purple-brown moorland. There was a fresh breeze, that put a nice chop on the water – just right for fishing – and I had some good sport catching two sea-trout, one a fresh silver fish, the other rather stale and coloured, but both well over 2 pounds, and a brown trout of about a pound. While I was playing the latter, we noticed that a pall of cloud had come down like an extinguisher on the great cone of Ben Stack, far down the loch to the north-west, and huge, dark-bellied clouds seemed to be welling up out of the hills all around us, smothering the tops and draining the scene of colour. Even as I slipped my net under the fish, a squall of thin, driving rain hit us and within a few minutes, as stronger gusts followed, deep indigo waves were coursing up the loch, with white horses curling at their crests. We made for our mooring as fast as we were able, and a bumpy, wet and uncomfortable ride it was, with the wind howling overhead, the boat pitching violently across the waves, and the rain and spume drenching us to our skins.

Although I am never loth to go fishing by myself, or at least with my dog for company, it does, I think, pay to have a human companion when fishing from a boat. I have never yet caught a loch salmon, but might have done so had I not rejected the chance of a boatman on one occasion. We were fishing the River Borgie, in the north of Sutherland, towards the latter end of the season, and though the river teemed with fish, they were as obstinately uncatchable as only salmon can be when they have a mind. Every fair means had been tried to entrap them, and worms in particular were much in demand, but at the end of a fortnight not a fish had been taken. The ghillie in attendance on our party was a charming old man called Murdo. He was assiduous in carrying one's rod, landing net and other gear – something I was quite happy to do for myself – but being in reality a retired stalker, he had very little notion about fishing, and he became famous for his reaction when shown a fly box and asked which fly he would recommend. 'Aye,' he would say, 'they're all verra nice flies,' and he would then pick out at random one which was often palpably unsuitable. I had decided, one day, to have a go on Loch Slam, the first and smallest of a chain of lochs that fed into the Borgie. Just as I was setting out, Murdo appeared and offered his services; thinking that I would prefer to be on my own, I thanked him but suggested that he waited for another guest, who was due to arrive at any moment and would probably want to go straight down to the river.

Arrived at the loch, I launched the boat and started a series of drifts, fishing for trout. The loch being small and a fresh breeze blowing, the drifts did not take long, but I enjoyed the work and may even have caught one or two small trout – I forget now. Then I saw a salmon rise – a nice head-and-tailer – and trout were forgotten. I debated whether to change my cast, but fearing lest the fish should move away while I was so engaged, I decided not to. Instead I took the oars and rowed the few yards or so that put me in a position from which I could cover the rise. I cast, and hey presto! The fish took first time. I could hardly believe my luck and chortled at the idea of bringing back the first salmon of the fortnight. The fish ran and the reel sang, then it came back and dived deep beneath the boat, and then ran again making a wide half-circuit around the boat's stern. Even with the light trout cast, there was no reason why I should not land it in time, if I was careful. I kept a good pressure on it, and after about ten minutes it began to tire and I saw it moving slowly just beneath the surface. But then I looked round and saw that we were drifting into a shallow bay full of rocks. How I wished at that moment that I had accepted Murdo's offer. Further up the loch there was a sandy inlet which would have been an ideal place from which to land the fish, but while I was playing it there was no way I could get the boat there. I looked around for an anchor, but there was none to be seen and we drifted on, the bows of the boat bumping gently against the rocks. I got the net ready and brought the fish towards me, but as it saw the net for the first time it turned away. The dropper fly (it had taken the Greenwell on the point) embedded itself in a rock, there was a sharp jerk on the line, and the next moment I was watching the fish weaving between the rocks and gathering speed as it headed back towards the deep water. I don't think I have ever been so disappointed at losing a fish.

Red-throated divers – a familiar species to the loch fisherman.

A Lesson in Gaelic

Years ago I decided to teach myself Gaelic, and bought a book for the purpose. I suppose it was a kind of tribute to the fact that I have a special fondness for the traditionally Gaelic-speaking parts of Scotland, in particular the north-western seaboard and the Hebridean islands. I never got very far with it, as bouts of learning were apt to be spasmodic, generally inspired by an imminent visit to the region, and between times I tended to forget most of what I had learnt, so I was always having to start again from the beginning. However, it was partly a desire to visit a place where the language was still generally spoken that made me pick on the Isle of Lewis, one summer, for a week's trouting, prior to staying with friends further south.

In fact I met my first Gaelic speaker before ever I reached Lewis. I arrived at the Kyle of Lochalsh too late for the Stornaway ferry and turning back found a pleasant little hotel at the head of Loch Alsh. There I spent a merry evening in the company of, among others, an Irish doctor from Glasgow who had been on his way to a retreat at Elgin but had unaccountably been prompted to take the road to the Isles instead, and an old stalker named Farquar who had some Gaelic and instructed me, among other things, in the correct pronunciation of Glen Morangie, with the stress, as in nearly all Gaelic words, on the first syllable. There was also a pretty barmaid whose surname was Lamont, the name of a small Argyllshire clan, who said she could never stop English people from pronouncing it La*mont* as if it had been a name of French origin. At the end of the evening, or what I took to be the end

of the evening, Farquar put his empty glass on the bar, sighed deeply, and addressing no one in particular, murmured, 'There's a ceilidh up the glen tonight.' He had a lovely, soft, lilting Highland accent.

A few minutes later I found myself at the wheel of my car with Farquar, the doctor, Jan the barmaid, a waitress and a young fellow called Jamie as passengers. 'Up the glen' proved to be a good 10 miles, but the ceilidh was worth it. I think I danced just about every reel. I was unfamiliar with most of them but willing hands whirled me around and shoved me in the right direction, and shouted instructions did the rest. It is surprising how quickly one can pick up the steps of a reel when everyone else knows them perfectly. The whisky kept flowing all evening but the violent exercise counteracted its effects and by the time the party ended I felt physically exhausted but relatively sober. Back at the hotel we all had one more, rather superfluous, drink and when I finally crawled into bed at about half-past five in the morning, I went to sleep with the strains of the last wild reel still ringing in my head.

Not many hours later, after an excellent breakfast, I walked down to the castle of Eilean Donan, and sat on the ramparts nursing a well-deserved hangover and contemplating the misty blue mountains across the still waters of the loch. In the afternoon I caught the car ferry to Stornaway, the waters of the Minch calm as a mill-pool throughout the four-hour crossing. I started to read a book but fell asleep and when I awoke we were gliding along beside the low, brown and rugged coastline of Lewis, while herring gulls held station beside us on rigid wings, and parties of shearwaters skimmed by over the barely rippled surface of the sea. From seaward the island seemed totally uninhabited and I thought I had never seen anywhere quite so desolate. Then we rounded a headland and there were the clustered grey roof-tops of Stornaway, the moored fishing boats, the jetties and all the colourful paraphernalia of a fishing port, every detail faithfully reflected in the oily-calm waters of the harbour. There was a smell of fish and seaweed and the air was filled with the raucous cries of innumerable gulls. Some fishermen were unloading their catch and shouting to one another in Gaelic, but I could not make out a single word that sounded remotely familiar.

There are said to be a thousand lochs on Lewis and for the modest price of a comprehensive licence the angler has the freedom of most of them. The month was June, the weather fair, and for five days I drove about the island and tramped many miles over the low, undulating hills of heather and rough grass, accompanied only by Danny, my dog. Every declivity ended in water, and with such an *embarras de richesses* it was difficult to know where to start. I would fish any water that I fancied the look of for half an hour or so, and if I stirred no fish, would move on to another. When fish were rising naturally, I generally got a take sooner or later, and sometimes I devoted a whole morning or afternoon to one particular loch. Most of the fish I caught varied between ½ and ¾ pound, and using my 9-foot Hardy cane rod and a 4X cast with two wet flies, I had excellent sport. On one day I had nine fish, and on another, despite fishing with equal zeal, and for no apparent reason that I could work out, only one, but no day was completely blank.

I think it was about the fourth day of my stay that I decided to explore some of the great expanse of wilderness that lies at the north end of the island. I drove up the coast road from Stornaway as far as Tolsta, where the road comes to an abrupt end, and set out on foot, Danny bounding ahead, flushing

meadow pipits from the heather and an occasional snipe from the boggy shores of a lochan. I saw surprisingly few birds, in fact, as I wandered about the island, only gulls gliding lazily, high overhead, a few hooded crows and once a raven flying purposefully towards the south-west as if bound for the distant mountains of Harris. Indeed, it was a rather dreary landscape compared with the more dramatic terrain of the nearest mainland: the low hills advanced like ocean swells, scoured and eroded by the winds and lashing rain of countless millennia. Ancient rocks and boulders, the debris of the last Ice Age, were scattered about their slopes and lay in jumbled heaps at the loch edges. But the water, snaking along valleys, filling small craters and bowls and flooding broad plains between the hills, gurgling in deep gullies through the peat or tumbling down rocky crevices in miniature cascades, gave life and sparkle to the scene, and from every eminence one could look out towards the deep blue of the sea and away to the humped and jagged outlines of distant milky-purple horizons. It was a day of soft, mild winds and fleeting grey clouds, which looked as if they might hold rain but never shed any, and fitful gleams of sunshine. Cloud shadows slid like drifts of dark smoke across the contours of the hills and there was a constant change of hue and intensity in the umbers and ochres of the moorland and on the loch surfaces which altered suddenly from glittering blue to dull pewter.

I must have walked 4 miles or more before I came to a smallish loch where the heather ran down to a sandy cove and the water was as pure and limpid as if it had just welled from a spring. Here I sat down on a springy couch of dry heather and ate my lunch of sandwiches accompanied by a bottle of beer. The only sounds were the lap of water, the faint threnody of the breeze through the heather and the faraway cries of gulls.

My lunch despatched, I decided there was no point in

Snipe feed in shallow water and in boggy ground.

walking on any further, and set up my rod and tackle, tying a Peter Ross on the point and a Zulu on the bob. Then I began to saunter around the perimeter of the loch, casting my flies out here and there as I went. I had walked right round one end of it and was clambering along the further shore which was fringed with rocks that formed a series of little bays and inlets, when I noticed that there were several trout rising. I cast towards one of them and got an immediate take, and by the way the reel sang as the fish charged towards the middle of the loch, I knew it was a good one. When it eventually stopped and jumped, it seemed an awfully long way away, and I could see that half the backing was off my reel. Fortunately, when it set off again, it chose a course parallel to the shore, and I was able, with some difficulty, to keep abreast of it and retrieve a little line. After that first spectacular leap, the fish did not show itself again for a long time, nor did it make another long run. It bored deep, and although I had it several times right at my feet, with the line going down almost vertically into the water, it kept out of sight. Attempts to bring it up provoked sullen, irresistible withdrawals towards open water. At last it did weaken though; I saw it moving listlessly, a dark shadow, down in the blue-green depths, and then quite suddenly it was floundering on the surface and in a moment I had drawn it over the net and lifted it from the water. It had taken the bob fly and was a lovely fish, small-headed, deep-bodied and weighing 3 pounds 2 ounces. It was then, and still remains, my biggest wild-caught brown trout.

While all this was going on I had noticed, out of the corner of my eye, a small figure making its way through the bog myrtle and asphodel at the head of the loch. Now I looked up and saw that it was a small boy, about seven or eight, with a shock of red hair and accompanied by a collie pup to whose collar he had just attached a length of string. He was making

A brown trout comes to the net on a Lewis loch.

his way towards me along the shore, and it occurred to me that this was the opportunity for which I had been waiting. Hitherto my efforts to improve my Gaelic had met with little success, since the people I had talked to in the hotel bar of an evening were mostly visitors like myself and I had felt too self-conscious to try out my faltering Gaelic on such native speakers as I had met – all of whom, of course, spoke perfectly good English. Now, however, I began to formulate an appropriate sentence in my mind, and as the lad drew near I greeted him with, 'Ciamar a tha thu?' He responded, and then, as he stood admiring the trout, I asked him, 'Carson nach eil thu anns an sgoil an diugh?' which I hoped meant, 'Why are you not at school today?' He replied with a gabble of unintelligible Gaelic, and it was a minute or two before he grasped the fact that my Gaelic was almost non-existent. By good fortune his command of English was not very much greater. At one stroke I had found myself not only a Gaelic tutor, but an excellent ghillie as well. When I started fishing again he insisted on holding my landing net, and all through the afternoon he stood at my side, out of the way of my back cast, eagerly following my progress, deftly landing my fish (he had obviously done it before), running to disengage my flies when I carelessly hooked the heather behind me and, once he realized that I wished to learn from him, teaching me more about the Gaelic language, in particular its difficult nasal pronunciation, than I had hitherto been able to acquire from hours of study. Our fishing was accompanied by yaps and growls from the collie pup, who was half-fearful of Danny but infuriated by the indifference he showed to his advances.

It was a wonderful afternoon's fishing. I caught seven fish in all, and although none of the others approached the first one in size, all but two were over a pound in weight. The delight of my self-appointed ghillie each time I hooked a fish, and his disappointment when I missed or lost one, as happened several times, infected me with a similar kind of boyish enthusiasm, reminding me that the intensity of pleasure in such simple pursuits as fishing is all too apt to become dulled with age.

Eventually the fish went off the take, and after I had fished on for an hour or more without getting any response, even my helper's interest began to wane, and he started throwing a piece of heather-root for the puppy to retrieve. I was more than content with my day's sport and since I had a long tramp back to the car, I decided to pack up my gear and head off across the moor. The boy indicated that his road lay towards the north-west. 'Beannachd leat agus tapadh leat,' I said, 'goodbye and thank you,' and we shook hands solemnly. For a long time I could see him, the black and white pup bouncing through the heather at his side, his mop of red hair flaring like a beacon, a diminishing figure in the midst of that trackless waste of heath, bog and water. When he was only a tiny dot on the crest of a distant hill, he turned and waved. I never did discover if he was playing truant from school, but if he was, I hope he got away with it.

A pair of scavenging hoodie crows on the loch-side.

Hill Lochs and Lochans

The narrow track seemed endless, clawing its way up the steep flank of the mountain in a series of acute-angled zigzags. Compared with the direct route, the gradients were gentle enough, but every step was upwards and before long I was breathing hard, and unaccustomed leg muscles were complaining bitterly. Coat and sweater were shed and their weight was added to the fishing bag slung from my shoulder which contained a packed lunch as well as fishing gear; the sweat ran into my eyes and the day seemed unnaturally hot. Once past the birch and bracken woodland that straggled a short way up the lower slopes, some relief was provided by a breeze that swept across the escarpment, fanning the bents into life, but the track now became tired of its leisurely progress and the sweeps to right and left grew markedly steeper. Horizons which seemed to promise an end to the climb were attained, only for new ones to appear in an apparently endless succession, but eventually, at about 1,300 feet, the ground began to level off, and I sunk down thankfully into the heather, facing the way I had come, and surveyed the scene spread out below me.

Tawny, purple and black, the ancient, gloomy hills of Sutherland rolled away until they merged with the clouds that were banked across the sky in ragged layers of pearly white and slate grey. They were hills scoured and abraded through many ages by ice and wind into humped and rounded shapes, their sharp edges blunted, their contours reminiscent now of couchant lions, prostrate horses and camels' humps. On their massive flanks, like fur on the hide of a mangy beast, the heather – not yet in flower for it was early in the year – formed random patches of purple-brown against the yellower areas of bog-grass, and from the valley bottoms conifer plantations, of a green so dark as to be almost black, spread up the mountainsides in hard-edged, unnatural configurations. Across the centre of this uncompromising landscape, Loch More lay like a length of grey-blue silk, dully reflecting the lighter tones of the sky, and beyond it the furthest mountains, their crests hidden by clouds, were pale grey silhouettes faintly streaked with the white of quartz screes that would glitter when the sun shone.

Now the sun was hidden, and not a patch of blue sky showed. I turned inland once again and followed the track which passed across a desolate terrain, pitted and rock-strewn, that fell away sharply on my right, and on my left climbed up among a jumble of boulders and rock outcrops, towards a misty summit. In time I came to an area – the highest point on a bleak plateau – where the track ended among a scattered group of cairns. No doubt they were visible from far afield, and provided a useful landmark in that trackless waste. I got out my ordnance survey map, and found the direction of the loch for which I was bound, though I was surprised to find that I could not actually see it from where I stood. Between it and me lay an area honeycombed with enormous black peat-haggs that gaped like toothless mouths. I started to make my way among them, but soon they became so numerous that it was like following the windings of a maze; I was getting nowhere, and I retraced my steps to the cairns and back along the track, deciding to descend the valley, instead, by way of the mountainside, where the going was rough but reasonably dry. From this angle, also, the loch was invisible, but I had noticed, when consulting the map, that it was called Loch Cul a' Mhill, and my scant understanding of Gaelic suggested that this meant 'the loch behind the hillocks'. So it proved to be, for after ½ mile of scrambling among rocks and stagnant pools full of black, crimson and green Sphagnum mosses, I climbed a slight eminence, and

there it was, suddenly right before me, an irregular-shaped sheet of leaden-hued, rippled water, with the hillside rising steeply along its eastern shore.

As I had made my slow ascent towards the plateau, the clouds had been lowering, and now they passed in a dismal procession overhead, less than a hundred feet above loch-level. The wind increased, bringing with it a thin rain and sending choppy wavelets across the loch to slap mournfully against its stony shore. I had long since resumed my sweater

Frog at the edge of a moorland pool.

and coat and now, turning up my collar and pulling the hood over my head, I decided to fortify myself with some sandwiches and a dram before starting to fish. As I sat down on a boulder and contemplated the scene before me, I had to admit that it would be difficult to conceive of a landscape more unmitigatedly drear and cheerless. For there is an inherent sadness about some of these highland landscapes, particularly when the terrain consists chiefly, over wide areas, of eroded and deeply dissected peat-bog, such as that that I had tried unsuccessfully to negotiate earlier. One has to remind oneself that despite its primeval appearance, much of this landscape was once covered by trees and scrub. Man it was who first cleared it and then the grazing animals, both wild and domestic, prevented the trees from growing again and the long process of soil deterioration set in. In such forlorn wastes one sees few creatures except for midges, frogs, the occasional moth or crane fly and the ubiquitous large black slugs, and the flora is dull, consisting principally of Sphagnum mosses and various species of grass, sedge and heather. I saw few birds – only some meadow pipits and hooded crows, a solitary heron and a pair of grouse – but a small herd of red deer hinds that I had disturbed from their grazing on the initial ascent kept moving ahead of me, climbing the hill that overlooked the loch with enviable ease, and stopping every now and then to look down at my awkward progress, until they were swallowed up in the mist.

Of fish I saw no sign, and with the surface layer of water ruffled by a keen breeze and whipped by flurries of thin, chilling rain, I decided to try to get my flies down as deep as possible. I mounted a sinking line, and with this, a size 12 Peter Ross on the tail and a 10 Black Pennell on the bob, I set to work. The day before, I had fished a loch in the hills on the far side of Loch More, where I had caught sufficient 6 to 7 ounce fish to provide our little party with a good breakfast the next morning. On the way back down the mountain track I had met, and had a few words with, a man who had recommended the loch I was now fishing as having fish of a larger overall size than most of the hill lochs in the area. Gazing at its inscrutable, dark waters, I had to kick myself, mentally, into believing that there were fish down there at all, let alone that they could be tempted into taking my flies.

The wind was blowing down the loch, but slanting in towards the shore that I was fishing. Behind me the heather slopes rose almost vertically towards the low ceiling of cloud, and the combination of wind and the heather so close behind me made casting anything but easy. Several times I had to lay down my rod and haul myself up the cliff to disengage hooks from wiry heather stems. These frustrating delays, the difficult nature of my progress along the edge of the loch and the fact that no fish showed any interest in my flies, almost made me decide, after about an hour, to give up and head for home. There was also a nagging worry in my mind: could I find my way back through the mist (which had now obscured even the far shore of the loch) and locate the narrow track which would lead me down the mountain? I had no desire to get lost in such an inhospitable wilderness. A bonus point was that the rain had now stopped, and the wraiths of mist that hurried overhead had come no lower and indeed seemed to be lifting slightly, for I would catch occasional glimpses of looming shapes ahead that would appear briefly, then vanish.

Then something occurred that put all thoughts of going home out of my head, mist or no mist: a movement on the water surface that was undoubtedly a fish. It was at the point of a rocky promontory that jutted out into the loch forming one of a series of little, enclosed bays that ran all the way down this side of the water. As the wind drove the hurrying wavelets past this point and in towards the shore, a small slick of foamy scum had formed on the sheltered side of the rock. It moved in a kind of sluggish spiral, and no doubt attracted and held any passing flotsam that came close enough to be pulled into its orbit. It was here that the fish had risen, and presently it rose again.

Within a few minutes I had changed my sinking line for a floater, and having attached the same cast and flies that I had been using before, I looked around for a position from which I could cast across the slick. It was not easy, for the whole littoral of the loch was a mass of rocks and boulders of all sizes, some fixed, others loose and often precariously balanced. I also found I had to cast across the wind, and at my first attempt a gust caught the flies in mid-air and landed them in an ugly loop well downwind of where I had intended them to go. The next cast was more successful, and at about the fourth cast I was rewarded with a strong pull. The line zipped through the water, and the fish leapt. It was an active fish, and powerful for its size, but soon I had persuaded it into the bay and over the landing net – ¾ pound. With all my keenness for the fray restored, I continued my scrambling progress down the loch, stopping at each little bay that I came to and fishing, wherever possible (sometimes it was quite impossible), towards the foam-slicks in the lee of projecting rocks. At one place I was able to cast directly downwind and reach the desired area with my flies, by casting over the top of a large, flat rock, and this produced a nice fish of just under a pound, which fought very fiercely. I also caught another fish of just under the ¾-pound mark, and a small one which I returned, but I lost one other good fish after playing it for more than five minutes.

During this time the cloud layer had risen considerably, and distant mountains had come into view again. There had even been a brief period during which a wan glow of sunlight had forced its way through the gloom and put a sparkle on the water. But by the time I had reached the far end of the loch, the clouds were descending once more, the thin rain had resumed and I decided to pack up. Having negotiated the obstacle course back along the edge of the loch, my doubts returned in full force as I started off along the side of the

Fishing a high lochan in Angus.

mountain with visibility, by now, reduced to 20 yards at the most. The worst point came when I had to leave the sloping ground and strike out across the open plateau towards the track. There was the pool with the patch of bright crimson Sphagnum that I had noticed on the way out, and the large rock with the smaller boulder balanced on top; there was the shallow burn I had to cross and the peat-hagg full of frogspawn coated with green algae – but after that there were no more remembered landmarks, and when I had walked considerably further than I felt I should have done, the ground began to slope precipitously, and I knew that I had gone wrong. Fighting down an incipient feeling of panic, I turned round and began to walk back very slowly, staring at the ground in front of my feet. Even then I almost missed the track for a second time. It was only about 18 inches wide and with such a short section visible could all too easily be overlooked. Once on it I heaved a sigh of relief, and set off down the hill. Within a few hundred yards I had left the mist behind me, and by the time I reached the top of the birch wood it was just an ordinary, rather grey, mid-May day. The desolate upland, under its pall of cloud, was another world.

Hill lochs among high peat-bogs seldom yield trout of any size, and some are so profoundly acid and lacking in nutrients as to be quite barren of fish, particularly those that lie over a granite bedrock. Occasionally, however, some quirk of the local geology will result in a sweeter, greener type of loch, where the fish thrive and grow to greater average sizes than those in neighbouring lochs. The chance discovery of such a loch is always an exciting event but even near-barren lochs over bedrock, or peaty lochs where fish abound but never grow to any size, can sometimes produce surprises. I remember fishing a very dour loch, once, where the water was as brown as strong tea and the bare rocks fringing it offered little hope of any kind of nourishment for whatever inhabited it. I had fished for an hour or two without stirring a fin, and was on the point of abandoning what appeared to be a fruitless exercise, when I remembered that I had, in my fishing bag, a very small Mepps spoon. On an impulse I replaced the light cast I was using with a length of strong nylon, tied on the Mepps, and with mental apologies to my abused rod as the back cast produced a horrible twanging sound, threw the little spoon as far out as I could get it, let it sink a few feet and then began to retrieve it. After four or five more casts I was watching the dull flash of gold approach me through the murky water when my heart almost stopped as I perceived a dark shadow in hot pursuit. It seemed enormous and as it turned away at the last moment I had visions of catching a veritable monster. At the next cast I had a fierce take almost immediately. A dour, deep struggle followed, but eventually I persuaded to the surface, and netted, a fish that was a monster only in the sense of being the ugliest trout I had ever caught. It weighed 2 pounds 2 ounces but was inordinately long for its weight, very lean, very black and with a pronounced kype. I had the feeling that it was the last trout in the loch, slowly starving to death after having devoured all its brethren.

More often, the compensations for a lack of trout or an over-abundance of very small fish are provided by sights and sensations beyond, rather than below, the water's surface – with the climb up into the hills, the changing scenery and chance sightings of birds, beasts and interesting plants. I saw my first golden eagle when fishing a lochan in the hills of Easter Ross. Till then I had often seen distant buzzards and debated whether they might be eagles, but when the real thing came gliding across the face of the mountain opposite me, on imperious, outstretched wings, I knew I would never be bothered by such indecision again. Since then I have several times seen eagles when fishing in remote hills, and the sight never fails to thrill. The last occasion was last summer when I was fishing at the head of the River North Esk, in Angus. The river was low and the salmon stale, and there seemed little point in fishing it seriously unless a good spate

came along to freshen things up. There had been some thunderstorms during the night, but insufficient rain had fallen to affect the water level to any significant degree, and after fishing for an hour or two in the early morning I decided, after breakfast, to try for trout instead.

The North Esk flows out of Loch Lee and during the morning I caught two or three trout from its shores. In the afternoon I fished first the little feeder stream at the head of the loch. In the glassy shallows where it flows towards the loch through rushy flats close-cropped by rabbits and sheep, numerous trout were rising. I put on a greased cast and a small dry Greenwell, rose and missed a great many, and finally caught a ½-pounder. Then I decided to make for a hill loch a mile or two back up the glen. It was during the ascent that I saw the eagles, two of them, soaring in lazy, effortless circles high above the glen and away down the loch-side and over the lodge towards the blue shimmer of distant hills.

The loch for which I was headed lay in the corner of a little plateau of high moorland, and in the shadow of a semi-circular wall of rock that towered up some 300 feet. It lay in a dip and did not become visible until I was within a few hundred yards of it – an oval pool of dark water, towards which the heather sloped gently down, vanishing quite suddenly with no intermediate zone of reed, sand or shingle. Fish were rising all along its near shore as I arrived, and after fishing for about forty minutes I had taken two of them – very black fish of just under ½ pound and rather lean. Then the rise ceased quite abruptly, and after that I fished for some time without making any further contact. Eventually I laid down my rod, and began to explore one of the water courses that ran down the cliffs, looking for flowers and ferns.

Blue hares abounded and my young dog had an ecstatic time vainly pursuing them. They eluded her with contemp-

Bringing a trout to the net on a small loch in the hills above Loch More.

tuous ease, either vanishing into caverns beneath the massive boulders that lay in heaps at the foot of the cliff, or quickly gaining height, then standing on their hind legs and calmly looking down on her as, nose to ground, she laboriously followed their scent. From the cliff-tops I could hear the croaking of ravens and around the top of a pinnacle that rose from the far end of the loch, a family of four peregrines were at play, screaming and stooping and chasing each other in a virtuoso display of aerobatic skills. I found no plants of special interest beyond a few tufts of alpine lady's-mantle and a solitary specimen of roseroot, but got so carried away by my quest that when I eventually looked down towards the loch, I found I had climbed much higher than I had intended, and was overtaken by an attack of vertigo that made me cling very tight, for several minutes, to the nearest piece of rock – I have a poor head for heights! I had registered, however, that the surface of the loch was once again decorated with the spreading rings of rising fish, and presently I had recovered my equilibrium sufficiently to commence a cautious descent. Another hour and a half's fishing produced a further brace of little black fish, which on my lightweight tackle gave a good fight; then thoughts of a hot bath and dinner began to beckon, and packing up my gear, I headed off across the moor, well satisfied with my day. As I trudged through the heather, ring ouzels – large, black thrushes with white crescents on their breasts – rose and flew ahead of me, uttering alarm calls not unlike those of fieldfares; there were perhaps twenty-five or thirty of them in all. Half-way down the hill I disturbed a roe buck which bounded through the heather in graceful, flying leaps at my approach, and vanished into the woodland among the tall boles of spruces and Scots pine below me.

Occasionally, in the Highlands of Scotland, one may be lucky enough to come across a loch or group of lochs where limestone outcrops through the predominant metamorphosed granite, providing sweeter water, more food and consequently better – sometimes much better – trout. Well-known

and a wonderfully green and pleasant place it is. Since limestone is good for flowers as well as fish, I spent at least as much time botanizing as fishing, but an afternoon on the small loch near my friends' house quickly produced as many trout as we needed for supper – only ½-pounders, but plump, handsome little fish, and very ready takers. A morning spent on a larger loch, set among low, green hills in the centre of the island, gave a hint of what might have been, had I spent more time fishing and less flower-hunting. I had not made arrangements to take out the boat, so was forced to fish from the shore, and a strong wind blowing straight up the loch made it very difficult to cast beyond the reeds that grew in the shallows all around the bank. I was not wearing waders, and most of my time was taken up in trying to find a promontory from which I could cast to open water. I had only one take, but it was from a very large trout. It gave me a few moments of intense excitement as I felt the power of its run and heard the reel sing, but then it swirled on the surface and my fine cast was snapped. I was granted no second chance!

Stonechat on gorse.

examples are the magnificent Durness lochs and various waters in Caithness and Orkney, and shell-sand provides similar conditions for the machair lochs on the western coasts of the Outer Hebrides. Several years ago I spent a few days staying with friends on the little island of Lismore that lies between Mull and Appin. The whole island is of limestone

The Great Salmon Rivers

Scotland can boast four rivers that merit the appellation 'great': Spey, Tay, Tweed and the Aberdeenshire Dee. Put them in whatever order you like (and all have their vociferous champions), each provides salmon fishing of the very first quality even when compared with bigger and more prolific rivers in, say, Norway or North America. In England and Wales most of the large rivers have fostered the growth of sprawling conurbations and industrial complexes upon their banks, and since the onset of the Industrial Revolution early in the last century, have become too polluted to allow the passage of migratory fish. Only the Herefordshire Wye (also, in part, a Welsh river) can claim to be in the same league as the great Scottish rivers.

One of the most obvious disadvantages of being a holiday fisherman is that one is entirely dependent upon the vagaries of the climate. The fortunate man who lives within striking distance of a river can plan his outings to coincide with propitious river conditions but the holiday fisherman must make his plans in advance and can only hope that he will hit it lucky. Generally, our climate being what it is, he does not; hence all those excuses that non-fishermen find so boring about the water being too high or too low or at the wrong temperature, the wind being too strong or else non-existent, and so on. In fact it is very seldom indeed that all the elements concur to produce conditions that are anywhere near perfect, and even when they do the cooperation of the salmon can never be guaranteed. Their motivations, despite the research that has been endlessly lavished upon them by generations of anglers, are still very often shrouded in the deepest mystery.

These two factors – unpredictable climate and unpredictable behaviour on the part of the fish – robbed me of what ought to have been two outstanding weeks' fishing on the only occasions that I have had the opportunity to fish, respectively, the Wye and the Tweed.

My invitation to fish, with four friends, an excellent beat on the Wye, followed upon a week when twenty-two salmon had been caught, so we were full of eager anticipation when we foregathered on the river bank on the afternoon of June 1st. Most of the fish caught hitherto that season had been taken on the spinner, but the ghillie reckoned that the water was coming right for fly, and I accordingly put up a fly rod. We all started fishing with that nervous haste with which one often starts a fishing holiday, setting up one's gear with fumbling fingers, at breakneck speed, and almost running down to the water's edge as if the loss of even half a minute is bound to lose one a fish. But there was an ominous stillness in the air and large, amorphous, sickly hued clouds were gathering overhead. We saw salmon, but they showed no interest in either fly or spinner. I did, however, catch a fish, and a fish that puzzled me considerably. It was of a silvery colour, with no markings, but with a faint pinkish tinge on its flanks. It had a deeply forked caudal fin, no adipose fin, a long but narrow anal fin, and weighed about 1¼ pounds. I returned it to the water, but later described it to Len, the ghillie, who told me that it was a shad. The shads are uncommon and little-known fish that, like salmon and sea-trout, come into

fresh water to spawn. There are two British species, but this one, from the fact that it was caught so far upriver and had no markings on its flanks, must have been an allis rather than a twaite shad.

The shad provided the only compensation (admittedly a very small one) for what happened next. We had enjoyed a good dinner and a convivial evening at our comfortable inn and had gone to bed still full of hopes for the morrow. During the night we were awoken by the grumblings of thunder, soon accompanied by the drumming of heavy rain. We came down to breakfast worried, but still hopeful that conditions might not be too bad; perhaps, we told each other without much conviction, it was only a local storm. But when we arrived at the fishing hut, Len's face, and a sight of the river coming down in a raging flood the colour of milky coffee, said all. Len assured us that it would take four days to clear, and we had no alternative but to pack our gear and head for home. Later we heard that in the following week, with the water fining down after the flood, another catch in excess of twenty fish was made. Someone has to get the short straw but why, one is tempted to ask, does it always have to be me?

Of course it doesn't and isn't – it only seems like that at times. My visit to the Tweed was made in February, and for

A typical Speyside scene: woods and pastureland near the river, mountains in the distance.

the whole week, not only was the weather quite pleasant for the time of year, but the water was in perfect condition. It was falling after a flood when we arrived; early in the week we were rained off for one day and thereafter the river was again falling and clearing – we couldn't have asked for anything better. My companion, Barry, and I had both been invited by a good friend who, sadly, had become ill at the last moment and had been unable to join us. We were fishing the Lower Floors Castle beat, and when we arrived at the river we were met by the two ghillies who soon apprised us of the catch in what seemed to be an ideal scenario for success. Apparently the news of the river's perfect condition had not reached the salmon. The smaller and older of the ghillies, who had charge of me for the week, shook his head gloomily. 'Aye,' he said, 'the river's just fine. The trouble is, there are nae fush, nae fush at all; even the nets are havin' a lean time of it.' And so it proved. Day after day we bobbed about in the boats, sitting like a couple of garden gnomes on the high, mushroom-shaped fishing seats in the sterns, sending our spinning baits flashing over the water and reeling them in until our wrists and shoulders ached, and all we caught were kelts. Sometimes we saw what the ghillies assured us was a clean fish, but such sightings were few and far between. The kelts at least relieved the monotony of the proceedings, for casting a spinner all day from a sitting position can come to seem rather like hard work. Sometimes there was a chance to stretch one's legs and do a bit of bank fishing, and one day, when there was a strong blow, the ghillies forsook their oars and played the boats out on ropes, which they controlled from the bank.

I had brought with me a new 14-foot fly rod, which I had borrowed from a friend and was eager to try out, and although the ghillies insisted that our chances were much better spinning, I was not entirely convinced by their logic. I had noticed a nice piece of fly water a little way upstream from the fishing hut, where it was possible to wade, and I determined to devote at least one afternoon to fishing it with the fly. It was pleasant to be on my own for a change and, after so many hours of mechanically flicking out and reeling in Devons, the supple action of the big rod, even with a heavy fly attached, was a delight.

The water sparkled in the pale February sunlight, and a flotilla of swans sailed past me, haughty, graceful and immaculately white. On the steep bank opposite, snowdrops were flowering in huge drifts among ash and sycamore boles, and behind me open parkland studded with the bare, sepia outlines of ancient trees sloped upwards to where, on the horizon, the great ducal house of Floors surveyed the scene, its windows flashing fire from the low beams of the sun.

I was wading slowly down a long spit of gravel, casting with every pace and covering the water very thoroughly, and had been doing this for a quarter of an hour or so, when I got a good, firm take. When I tightened, the fish made a long dash across the river and then rolled on the surface, sending up a fountain of spray as it flailed angrily with its tail. Feeling the power of its initial run, and the buck of the rod as it took off again downstream, I felt a surge of elation. This, surely, must be a salmon at last. All the time I played it I had a triumphant feeling inside me – the first clean salmon of the week, a big one at that, and caught on the fly. So much for all their theories about spinning being the only way to catch a fish at this time of year! But although the fish fought gallantly, I did wonder that it tired quite so soon, and when eventually I got it to the bank, my heart sank as I bent over it and examined it carefully. That tinny brilliance on its flanks – not quite the silvery gleam of a fresh fish, those frayed pectorals, a spongy feel to its abdomen and the depth of its body not quite matching up to its length. 'Damn!' I cried, loud enough to alarm a passing coot, it was undoubtedly a kelt, though very well mended; without taking it from the water I slipped the hook from its jaw and eased it back into the current. It gave a wag of its tail and was gone. I reckoned that it must have been a fish of well over 20 pounds before spawning.

The River Tweed, near Kelso, in February.

On the Saturday morning, at the end of our week's holiday, once again under the discipline of the mushroom stool and the spinning rod, luck came at last both to Barry and to me. He was fishing the Weir Pool above the Junction, the bottom pool of our beat, and I was fishing the Island Pool, and we each had a salmon – 11 pounds and 8 pounds. No one could have mistaken those fresh-run spring salmon for kelts; they were steely-hard and bright as polished silver. Very possibly they were the vanguard of a big run, and the next week's fishing tenants would have a bonanza. I contemplated the prospect with a certain degree of sourness.

The only other of the major salmon rivers that I have fished is the Spey. It was on one of the beats below Grantown – I forget now the name of the water – that I first experienced the thrill of being in direct contact, via rod and line, with a salmon. The fish was landed, too, but I don't really claim it as my first salmon, since I was a complete tyro at the time and practically everything was done either by, or with the aid of, the ghillie who had been giving me some basic instruction in casting. That was a long time ago, and in the spring. Subsequent visits to the Spey have all been made at the back-end of the season, but I hope one day to have the chance again, and this time with rather more experience to aid me, to do battle with a Spey springer.

For the Spey is a queen among rivers. It winds majestically between woodlands and rich pastures through a wide valley bounded by hills, and the travelling fisherman stopping almost anywhere along its course yearns to be able to set up his gear and cast his line across its delectably streamy waters. Anyone driving between Grantown and the sea should follow the old road, on the north bank of the river, rather than the A95, at least if he has time to spare. The road frequently follows close beside the river, and one is continually being tempted to stop the car and stand awhile, entranced by the sparkling, swift flow of the water and the fish that disport themselves, so frustratingly unattainable, on its surface. I spent several hours doing just that one fine August day last summer, and I have never seen so many fish showing. In the Manse Pool below the iron bridge at Cromdale the activity was so great that I was able, in the space of about twenty minutes, to take half a dozen photographs of jumping fish, just by pointing my camera at a patch of water and waiting for one to show. Whether these would have been taking fish or not is another matter. The fisherman – I think he was a Dutchman – who had the water that afternoon apparently did not think so, for after strolling slowly up and down the bank, he laid down his rod, lay on his back in the grass and, to all appearances, went to sleep! Either he had had a surfeit of fish

already or, perhaps more likely, he had become dispirited by their lack of interest in his offered lures. Alternatively he may have been shy at the thought of performing before a row of onlookers, for a dozen or so people were gathered on the bank, attracted by the leaping salmon.

I know I should not have been able to show such a blasé attitude towards all that piscine activity. Maybe such a frenzy of jumping did not denote the likelihood of fish being in a taking mood, but I could never have convinced myself of the truth of such a negative view; in any case I would have assumed the presence, beneath the surface, of a body of staid, imperturbable fish, ready to notice and resent the sight of my fly flickering past their noses. The more so on this particular pool, because I had memories of catching a salmon there, almost under the bridge, several years before. On another occasion when my turn had come round to fish the Manse Pool, the water was running very high and coloured, and after an unproductive spell with the spinning rod, fly fishing being out of the question under prevailing conditions, I had set the rod aside and taken my dog for a run along the bank downstream. Presently I came to an area of slack water in the lee of some large boulders where I noticed that there were a lot of trout rising to a hatch of iron blues. I went back to my car, set up a dry fly rod and soon had two nice yellow trout on the bank, each over a pound, besides missing several others.

It was during that same September week, when I was fishing a pool ½ mile or so below the Manse, that I observed a strange phenomenon: a man was wading up the opposite side of the river, bent over and holding to his eye a tube, the end of which was in the water. I couldn't imagine what he was doing, but enquiry of the ghillie solicited the information that he was searching for pearl mussels. Later I came across several of these large bivalves which occasionally contain pearls of a good size and considerable value. There used to be a regular commercial pearl fishery, said to have been worth thousands of pounds a year in the mid-eighteenth century, but the

process is a wasteful one since many shells have to be opened, thereby killing the animal, for every pearl that is found.

Another species that was new to me I encountered while walking in the woods behind the lodge where we were staying. These woods were full of huge and ancient Scots pines as well as birches, aspens and junipers, and were, I imagine, a remnant of the great Caledonian Forest that once covered most of the Scottish Highlands. From the top of a tall pine I put up first one and then, at intervals as I continued up the track, a dozen more large, turkey-like birds, which I recognized as capercaillies. Each burst out of the tree with a clatter, then set its wings and went gliding down over the tree-tops, a most impressive sight. These very large game birds became extinct in Britain in the mid-eighteenth century, but were successfully re-introduced during the nineteenth century, and are now rather precariously established in the parts of Scotland where there remain tracts of the kind of open coniferous forest which they favour.

On my latest visit to the Spey we were fishing the Kinchurdy water, above Grantown. On the first morning I was fishing on my own at the bottom end of the beat, near Boat of Garten, and walking down towards the river along a track bordered by juniper bushes and small rowan trees, I stopped to watch a pair of red squirrels chasing each other among the branches of the trees that stood back from the track on my right. I thought sadly of the day when these charming small animals were common in the Essex village where I then lived. They disappeared quite suddenly when the greys arrived about 1960, and now I seldom see any south of the Scottish border. I did not stop for long, though, for the river beckoned imperiously; broad and swift, with the streamy rock-strewn character that is typical of so much of the Spey, it was a lovely sight. Bordered by clumps of wych-elms, birches and bird cherries, rowans richly bedecked with clusters of

The dipper is found on nearly all swift-flowing rivers.

orange-scarlet fruit, and aspens whose leaves had already turned a clear, creamy yellow, its waters flashed and glittered in the mellow September sunlight. I started fishing where a line of stepping stones ran out obliquely from the shore. There had been rain and spates during the previous week, and nine fish had been caught by my host's party, all on spinner. But now the water had been falling for several days, and was perfect for fly. I put on a treble of my own tying and doubtful identity – crimson-bodied with silver ribbing and a black hair-wing and hackle – and got to work. Before I had reached the end of the stepping stones I had landed a fish of 7 pounds, and within twenty minutes of starting to fish again, another of 9 pounds, both of them cock fish. Such a start to a week's fishing is heady stuff; it put me in a mood of high exhilaration, and when we all foregathered further upriver for lunch, I found that two others of the party had caught fish, both on spinners. But as it turned out, that was to be the end of the action for the best part of the week. By next morning the river had fallen to its summer low and none of our party, or of those fishing from the opposite bank, caught any fish. It was not until our last day's fishing, which was on a Friday, that things took a turn for the better. There had been rain in the hills the previous night, and its effects were beginning to show on the upper part of the beat. Unfortunately for me I was fishing again where I had started at the beginning of the week, and neither I nor the rods opposite had any luck, although I had one take in the late afternoon, the contact lasting only for some thirty seconds. Upriver, however (the top of the beat was 4½ miles from where I was fishing), it was a different story. A guest who had recently arrived and who, despite much trying, had failed to catch a salmon for the past eight years, broke the jinx and caught one in the morning and another in the afternoon, and my host's stepson, aged nineteen, caught four. Two were hens heavy with spawn which, at the ghillie's suggestion, were returned, but the other two were cock fish, one of them a splendid 18-pounder.

Small is Beautiful

Since I seldom have the opportunity of fishing the largest and most prestigious of salmon rivers, it is perhaps as well that my preference is really for the more intimate surroundings of less majestic waters. I confess that wading up to my armpits in a strong current over large boulders with only the unsteady support of a wading stick as insurance against a fast, involuntary passage downriver, is something I am quite happy to leave to those more daring and more agile than myself. My ideal is a river most of whose water can be covered either from the bank or by wading thigh-deep. One can acquire, over several visits, a very precise knowledge of the topography of such waters, learning just where the salmon and trout lie according to the height of the water. When summer drought bares the river's bones, you see rocks and boulders, deep pots and shingle banks, which are invisible and unsuspected when the water runs high and coloured, but which give valuable clues as to where fish might lie in such conditions, and sometimes, given clear water and an absence of surface glare, one can pick out, with the aid of Polaroid glasses, all the fish in the pool. No doubt long acquaintance with a large river results in a similar accumulation of knowledge, but more time is needed, and to a stranger the first sight of a river where the pools are as big as lakes, can be daunting, if there is no one at hand with local knowledge, who can advise on which parts repay careful fishing and warn against wasting time on unproductive stretches.

The salmon's world.

The first salmon that I hooked, played and landed alone and unaided was on the River Stinchar in Ayrshire, many years ago. It was towards the end of September, perhaps early October, for I have a picture in my mind of gold and russet foliage among the riverside trees. I was travelling with a friend, and we had obtained only one day's fishing, so we were lucky that during the night the rain came pelting down, providing a flash flood as if in answer to our prayers. When we reached the river after an early breakfast it was in full spate and the colour of old ale, but by mid-morning the water was already falling and clearing. I can still remember the intense excitement of the take: the solid, determined pull, followed by what seemed a surge of irresistible power as the fish moved steadily away. It was the first time I had seen my old, inherited, greenheart rod arch in earnest, and I was anxious lest long years of disuse had made it brittle. The fish took me a long way downriver and gave me several moments of heart-stopping panic, before it showed the gleam of its flank on the surface and I was able to coax it over the net. It was a fine example of the 'grey back' salmon for which the Ayrshire and Galloway rivers are famous, and at 17 pounds remains to this day my largest salmon.

A consequence of fishing smaller rivers, particularly the little spate rivers of the West Highlands and the Hebridean islands, is that the salmon are likely to be on the small side, often averaging between 5 and 8 pounds. A fish of 12 pounds or over, on such rivers, is a big fish, but a salmon's a salmon, and if it is a fresh-run fish and fights well, size is of little

importance. I dream, not infrequently, of catching a really big fish, or even a moderately big fish, but if the dream is never realized, so long as the occasional salmon, of whatever size, comes my way, I shall not repine.

That day on the Stinchar was one of those occasions when everything went right. More often, as I have noted before, things do not go so swimmingly for the fisherman who has to travel far and plan his fishing holidays well in advance. High and dirty water can inhibit fishing, but at least there is the prospect of the water fining down and producing excellent conditions eventually. Much more depressing, to my mind, is the sight of a river reduced to a miserable trickle under a cloudless sky, with half its bed exposed, the boulders and shingle bleached white by the sun. How one scours the heavens, each day, for any sign of a dark cloud and prays for mist to shroud the mountain-tops!

Last year, on the North Esk, was like that. There were compensations, of course, in fishing the lochs for trout and in splendid walks over the hills, with time to watch peregrines, eagles and red deer and to search for alpine flowers among the mountain screes, and especially in the sight of an osprey flying along the river one early morning, but days spent on the attenuated river were full of frustration. There were salmon present, but they were long-time residents, set in their ways and totally oblivious to the attractions of feather and tinsel. At the head of one pool, where a much-reduced stickle provided a little haven of oxygenated water, two fish were rising with great regularity, as stale fish will: a small fish of 5 or 6 pounds, and a larger, very red, cock fish of perhaps 10 pounds. I saw the latter's ugly kype very clearly on one occasion, when I was casting across the stickle, as he jumped clean over my floating line, in what seemed like a meditated gesture of contempt.

This year, travelling up the Great North Road early in July,

Low water conditions on the River North Esk, Keenie.

it seemed that low water and stale fish – if fish there were at all – would once again be our portion. It had been by no means a blazing June, but there had been little serious rainfall, and anxious attention to the weather reports from Scotland over several weeks suggested that it had been, if anything, even drier up there. Charlie and I were to fish the Deveron, in Banffshire, for the first week, and telephone calls to Robin, with whom we were to stay and who was to fish with us, confirmed our worst fears.

On the last leg of my journey I stopped at the top of Glen Shee to stretch my legs and give Islay, my dog, a run. We walked across the heather-clad hills for several miles and sat beside a tiny mountain burn where the rocks were bright with the flowers of yellow saxifrage, and I watched a gaily-coloured flock of hang-gliders soaring like huge, exotic birds, above the highest point of the glen. The sky was vivid ultramarine, across which small cumulus clouds drifted like galleons under full sail, and the air was deliciously warm.

Grey wagtail.

Continuing my journey I followed, first, the course of the Clunie Water, and then the Dee. They sparkled demurely in the sunshine, and like all the other rivers that I had passed since leaving home, they ran very low. When I reached the Deveron, it was the same story: I stopped in the village of Rothiemay to look over the bridge, and saw the river studded with dry rocks, its level scarcely reaching the first mark on the gauge. But then I looked up and my spirits lifted somewhat, for the puffs of cumulus were gone, and in their place a pale grey blanket of cloud was stretched across the sky. It was spreading fast, gobbling up the remaining patches of blue and in its further reaches was a slaty darkness that must surely bespeak rain.

Arrived at my hosts' house, I found Charlie already ensconced, whisky in hand, having set off from Lincolnshire in the early hours of the morning. As he poured me a generous dram, Robin told us that drought conditions had prevailed for five or six weeks, with hardly any fish being taken from the river. A very large salmon was reported to be in the Moses Pool, two local anglers claiming to have hooked and lost it, but of grilse or sea-trout there was as yet no sign.

That night it rained. The soft patter of the falling drops lulled me to sleep as sweet garden scents wafted into the room through the open window. If I dreamed, it must have been of salmon and sea-trout, for the omens now were good: a spate would surely bring fish up the river that had been waiting a long time for the right conditions to travel towards their spawning grounds.

The Deveron is a delightful river, flowing through a gently rolling countryside made up of a fairly even mixture of woodland, pasture and arable. As you walk along its banks in early July, there is the pleasant, faintly aniseedy, scent of sweet cicely. Gorse and monkey flower provide splashes of bright golden-yellow, and mixed with the tall reed-grasses are

The River Deveron, Mains of Mayen.

scarlet poppies, broad, creamy umbels of hogweed and the lovely purple-blue flowers of meadow cranesbill. I also came across several plants of large-flowered hemp-nettle, an uncommon species with striking pale yellow and violet flowers, and the alien and somewhat sinister giant hogweed that has invaded so many British rivers in recent years. One day I found the tracks of an otter in some mud beside the river, and was told by locals that otters had been increasing in recent years, which was excellent news. I grudge them none of the fish they catch, and in any event they probably do more good than harm by catching large quantities of eels. Birds included dippers, common sandpipers, numerous wagtails, both grey and pied, and there was nowhere along the river where the frenzied wheezing and warbling song of sedge warblers could not be heard. But the most insistent bird sound was provided by the oystercatchers: little parties of them were always chasing each other overhead or along the course of the river, and their frantic piping calls were the constant accompaniment to our fishing.

Robin and Charlie went out early, the morning after our arrival, but I stayed in bed and did not regret having done so when they returned at breakfast time to report the river still rising and very coloured. That day it was virtually unfishable, the peat-stained waters from the hills mixing with the silt-laden waters of the slow-flowing Isla to produce a thick and murky brew. By evening, however, it was beginning to clear and we fished for a couple of hours after dinner, though to no avail.

The next morning, Tuesday, the water was in perfect ply: falling, but not too rapidly, and of a lovely, amber colour, translucent now that the silty admixture from the Isla had dispersed. We heard that several fish, both grilse and sea-trout, had been taken at Turriff, some 15 miles downstream, and we fished with determination all day, though without getting any offers. I caught a couple of ½-pound brownies, which I returned, but the migratory fish apparently

had not yet arrived in the water. It is frustrating when the water looks so good, yet the fish are not there, but we knew it could only be a matter of time. Our worry was that the water would drop back too far before they arrived, but in fact it held its level well, assisted by occasional rain showers. Our first indication that the vanguard, at least of the sea-trout, had reached us, came on Wednesday and in a rather unexpected manner. The three of us had foregathered at the hut beside the Woodfold Pool to have our lunch, and had stayed there rather longer than we had intended, waiting for a heavy shower to pass by. When we emerged it was nearly half-past two; the sun was breaking through the clouds and the last drops of rain were pattering among the reeds at the river's edge. Charlie picked up a spinning rod of Robin's that was leaning against the eaves of the hut and a few words were exchanged concerning the old Ambassadeur reel with which it was equipped. 'Can I have a cast with it?' he asked. 'Sure,' said Robin and the 3-inch blue and silver Toby spoon was flicked across the river, plopping into the water a foot or two from the far bank. As the line came slowly across the glide at the pool tail, Robin and I stood watching. ''Be funny if he caught a fish!' we said almost simultaneously, and we were still chuckling at the thought when the line stopped and there was a boil on the surface of the water. 'By George, I think he's into one,' I cried. Robin grabbed the nearest landing net and slid down the steep bank into the river and a few minutes later netted out a fresh 2½-pound sea-trout, the first from the water for many a week. At 4.30 the same afternoon, fishing the Upper Trachore where a strong head of water flows into the top of the pool, I caught a similar fish of 2 pounds on a Teal Blue and Silver. Thereafter we all had some fun with sea-trout, most of the others being caught after dusk. Lovely fish they were too, the biggest 3½ pounds but none under 2 pounds. My most exciting fish I hooked at about eleven o'clock one evening. I lost it, in fact, but before escaping it gave a most spectacular display, first skittering very fast across the surface

of the pool right to the far side, then surging downstream before putting in a series of prodigious leaps. In the dim light of a summer evening, with the black water swirling past and tugging at my waders and the loud splashes of the fish resounding above the soft roar of the water foaming over the weir, it epitomized, for me, the special thrill of sea-trout fishing at night.

On Thursday afternoon, there was a tremendous thunderstorm. It started very suddenly, with a mighty clap of thunder that seemed to be directly above where I was fishing. I left my rod and other gear on the bank and, calling Islay, who had been happily rabbit-hunting while I fished, raced towards the car, which was a few hundred yards away. We reached it just in time, for presently we were engulfed in a deluge of rain. For an hour and a half the lightning flashed, the rain fell in an almost solid downpour, turning the steep farm track where I was parked into a tawny torrent, and the thunder, like a battle of Titans, rolled round and round the valley. That put paid to our fishing that night and for most of the next day, but the storm had fortunately been very local and by evening the water was clearing again and we were able to fish. Charlie stayed out all night and at five in the morning, fishing the run below Woodfold, claimed the first grilse, a lovely 6-pound silver fish with sea-lice still on it to testify to the speed of its ascent from the estuary, some 25 miles away. Alas, by then it was Saturday, and our last day on the river. During the morning I hooked, played for several minutes, and lost two grilse. I don't know why, perhaps I tightened into them too soon, but I was comforted by the fact that an ace local angler, who was on the same beat that morning, also lost two fish, although he landed a third. Our last fishing session was that evening. At about half-past eleven I was walking back down the river, picking my way carefully along the high bank where a careless step in the dark could easily land one in the river, and came upon Robin near the head of the Moses Pool. He was looking somewhat woebegone, and told me that he had

just lost a good sea-trout. 'Have another chuck,' I said. 'He might come again.' 'Oh, I don't know,' he answered. 'I've fished this piece of water pretty thoroughly now – still. . . .' He picked up his rod, got some line out and put his fly down somewhere in the darkness at the far side of the pool. I peered into the gloom, trying to make out the passage of his line across the water, when suddenly there was a high-pitched whine from the reel. 'Well, I'm dammed!' said Robin. I climbed down into the water, and after a few tense minutes, during which the fish leapt once, netted out a 2¾-pound sea-trout, rather long and lean and very heavily spotted. It made a nice end to our week on the Deveron.

From the Deveron Charlie and I went on to join other friends on the Moidart for a week. I had some business to attend to further north over the weekend, and did not arrive there until Monday evening. All the way down from Cape Wrath, from Ullapool to Muir of Ord, through the Great Glen to Fort William and along the beautiful coast road from Lochailort, it had rained solidly, with no let-up. Water poured off the mountains, burns and roadside ditches ran at full bore, every river was in spate.

Alastair, who had been fishing the river through the previous week, had had two grilse, but had had to work hard for them, for the river had been a trickle at the beginning of the week, and the only spate had been a half-hearted affair. Now we had what we all wanted, a full-blooded spate and a heavy, widespread rainfall, lasting a good 24 hours, that the mountain peat-bogs would absorb like sponges and release slowly into the rivers. Thus, even when the initial fury of the spate had abated, as it did quite quickly, the river maintained a good level, and throughout the week it was occasionally topped up by further falls of rain. For once we had hit the jackpot, for conditions were as good as they would ever be.

A pair of oystercatchers: their shrill piping accompanied all our Deveron fishing.

111

After the long weeks of drought, the estuary was full of fish eager to ascend the river. No doubt some of them went straight on up to the loch and beyond, but others tarried, and in no time at all the pools were full of fish. Ten salmon or grilse were taken from the lower river in the week, besides several that were hooked and lost, and all but one were fresh fish carrying long-tailed sea-lice. The exception was a fish that had been rising regularly through the week, in the same spot about half-way down the Dam Pool. It fell to Alastair's rod in the early hours of our last morning, and at 12 pounds was the largest fish of the week – a purplish-coloured hen fish with dark brown head and gills, it must have come into the river on some earlier spate.

That some fish do travel right up a river on a spate, while others may stay in the first pool they come to, is an obvious fact. Presumably this is partly due to the fact that there are only so many good lies, and if these are occupied late-comers will move on in search of *Lebensraum*. Some, indeed, go a very long way in the first dash, as was demonstrated by Charlie's Deveron fish, and fish with sea-lice still on them have been taken much further upriver than that. Perhaps the need to reach the spawning redds is more urgent in some fish than in others. However, there is a tendency to imagine that all fish have to go right up to the headwaters of the river in order to spawn, whereas in fact the first redds may be quite close to the sea, in a tributary burn, perhaps, or even in the main river. On the River Brora, for instance, the earliest spawning grounds occur immediately above the top tidal pool: ideal for the lazy salmon!

At any rate, all the pools on our stretch of the river were better stocked with fish than we had ever seen them. One day Charlie and I were standing by the March Pool, which is a narrow, deep and rocky gorge. The water was dark with peat-stain, but still clear enough to see the boulders on the bottom in all but the deepest parts. Fast-moving slicks and flecks of creamy foam on the surface made it difficult to concentrate one's gaze on the depths, and to begin with we could see no fish. Then I saw one move, and soon after Charlie pointed out another, and then a third. We donned Polaroid glasses and moved slowly up the pool. As our eyes accustomed themselves to the task we saw more and more fish, lying in serried ranks against the rock face on the far side, and no doubt there were more below us that we could not see. No hint of silver flanks showed, backs were perfectly camouflaged to match the boulders below and only the pale pectoral and pelvic fins gave their positions away.

The March Pool is a difficult pool to fish, but it was from here that what was probably the best fish of the week was taken. Robert, a guest at the castle, hooked it on a trout rod using a small Stoat's-tail, and it had been on for half an hour and had taken him some 200 yards downriver, involving a difficult scramble beside, and sometimes in, the water. It was lucky I came up the road at that moment for he had no net with him and had reached the head of the Cailleach where trees on the bank and deep pots under it would have made further progress impossible. The fish was in fast, broken water, and still very strong. To haul it back against the fierce current would have risked an almost certain break, and I urged him to hold it where it was while I got below it. It was an angry and determined fish, but eventually, having waded in as far as I was able, I got the net in its path as it came boring downstream through the choppy water, and scooped it up – a handsome, fresh cock fish of 9½ pounds.

In the evening the red deer come down from the hills to feed on the richer grazing beside the river.

Autumn Days on the Brora

The Brora, that runs into the sea at the little town of the same name on the east coast of Sutherland, is quite a small river, the best of its fishings being comprised in the 2 miles of water between its confluence with the River Blackwater and Loch Brora, and the 3 miles between Loch Brora and the sea. Size, however, is no arbiter of excellence, and the Brora provides sport of a quality that many a much larger river might envy. I have fished it on three occasions, all in late summer or autumn and as the guest of the same kind friends, and I think of it always with the greatest affection.

Looking back more than ten years, events tend to run together in the mind and their chronology becomes confused, but certain moments of excitement, interest or special enjoyment become etched in the memory, and these do not fade. In fact when I read my diary entries, however laconic, images come rushing back and I find that some sketchy memories remain of even the most uneventful days.

The lower River Brora, which we were fishing on my first visit, runs among hillocks and low cliffs where in late summer the grasses and rushes are tawny as a lion's mane and the bracken red as fire. Rowan trees are everywhere, bearing their heavy trusses of orange-vermilion fruit, and bottle-green gorse bushes scramble up every slope. Through this valley the river tumbles down, the cliffs sometimes receding so that it runs between flat swards of rough, sheep-nibbled grass, and sometimes closing in to form narrow gorges. Rapids or rocky runs provide the links between a series of delectable and characterful pools.

During that week it was my hostess, Stefa, who had the magic touch. She had already caught four fish the previous week and now, while the rest of us toiled away for a very occasional fish, she had only to cast her fly upon the water, it seemed, and the nearest salmon was after it in a trice. I remember a morning when I was fishing near the hut at the Madman Pool just before the 1.30 changeover. (Tenants on each bank of the river fish different halves of the water

morning and afternoon, thus ensuring that there are never rods fishing the same pool from either bank at the same time.) There were a few minutes still to go, and as Stefa joined me with the lunch I called to her that I had just felt a pluck and suggested that she came in behind me, and had a cast or two. She did so, was immediately taken and ten minutes later I landed a 7-pound fish for her. On another occasion she had a 15-pound fish with her first cast of the morning! By the end of the week I was still fishless and beginning to feel that the river gods were not on my side. Perhaps I should pour a bottle of the local Clynelish whisky into the water by way of a libation? I could think of nothing else, for I had been fishing with all the care and assiduity that I could muster.

On the last morning, since I was all packed and ready, it was suggested that I go down to the river for a last try and fish until Tim and Stefa (with whom I was travelling) picked me up at 1.30. I got a lift after breakfast with a departing guest, and walking upriver, started off at the long and stately pool known as the Bengie. Here I saw a fish rise to my fly, but it didn't take and I failed to rise it a second time. It was a beautiful October day, warm and sunny, and I noticed a couple of painted lady butterflies on the wing and wondered that they should have travelled so far north. I fished on down the river and came to two small pools called the Pots. The Upper Pot lies on the far side of a small island; below it the divided streams re-unite and in the cross currents that are created as they enter the Lower Pot one's line weaves and snakes on the surface and the fly presumably flutters and dances in an enticing manner. At any rate there was a sharp tug at my Hairy Mary, I tightened, and some fifteen minutes later tailed out an 8-pound salmon. From there I continued fishing down the rocky run known as the Cruives, and pausing only briefly at the Grilse Pool, came to the Magazine, a noble pool crossed obliquely by the headstream which then

The upper River Brora.

114

runs alongside a sheer sandstone cliff on the far side. Here I was soon doing battle with a rather larger fish, and having tired it, was drawing it towards the bank as Tim and Stefa drove into the yard of the old powder magazine which adjoins the pool and gives it its name. But the river gods obviously decided that they had relented sufficiently already, and at the last moment the hook came free and the fish turned slowly away and was lost to view.

A year or two later I hooked and landed my best Brora fish, a fresh and silvery 13-pounder, at precisely the same place, wading down from the head of the Magazine Pool. I also have bitter memories of an occasion when I was fishing at the tail of the pool and lost a fish, possibly two, through my own stupidity. I had noticed that my cast had acquired a wind knot, and searching in my bag found that I had only one spare cast left, which I attached in its place. Within a few minutes I had a take, but was almost immediately broken, the nylon parting just above the fly. I couldn't imagine how such a thing had happened, but vaguely assuming that it had come in contact with some sharp object under water, I tied on another fly, whereupon exactly the same sequence of events occurred. Only then did I think to test the nylon with my hands, when I found it was quite rotten and broke easily if I gave it a sharp jerk. It must have been a very old cast that had mouldered for years at the bottom of my fishing bag. Furious with myself, I drove quickly into Brora and purchased a new supply of casts, but returned only to find that a guest of the proprietor was standing on the bank a little way back from where I had been fishing, calmly playing a fish, with landing net at the ready. I did not wait to see whether it had either of my flies in its jaw, but stormed off up the river uttering imprecations under my breath. Needless to say, no more amenable fish came my way that day. I had, however, learnt a lesson, and since then have never kept any casts for more than a couple of seasons.

Mention of the Pots reminds me of an occasion when I was fishing the Upper Pot, which is reached by wading across a deep and strong stream and then fighting one's way across the little island which is crowded with bushes. The pool is very small, and can be covered by a few casts, but is said to be always worth a try. I have mentioned earlier that when fishing I often fantasize about the legendary monsters that have been caught – or hooked and lost – in the past. I was doing this now, and trying to imagine what it would be like to have such a fish as the record for the river – a mighty 45-pounder – at the end of my line, when the surface of the pool was broken by a gigantic dorsal fin and part of a vast back, followed by a great, black tail the size of a dinner plate. The impression of size was enhanced by the fish's proximity, for I could have touched it with the tip of my rod, and I was so taken aback that I retreated, with unsteady steps, to the bank, in order to regain my composure and consider my next move. While I stood there it rose again, this time showing a huge head, and I could have sworn that it leered at me for a moment and winked its fishy eye, before subsiding once more beneath the surface. With every allowance for possible exaggeration, it could not have weighed under 30 pounds, and I firmly believe that it was much nearer to the weight of that record fish that had been the subject of my reverie. I exchanged my small fly for a larger Garry Dog, as being more worthy of the attention of such a leviathan, and fished the pool out carefully, but of course with no result, and I saw it no more. Indeed, I wonder what would have happened if I had hooked it, stranded as I was on the little island, since I doubt if it would have tarried long in that small pool and flight in either direction would have posed grave problems.

It was on the Brora that I enjoyed one of the most exciting afternoons of all my fishing career. The morning had been hopeless, with the water running high and coloured, a howling wind that made casting virtually impossible and no fish showing. Stefa and I had had our lunch and were fishing at the Well Pool, when she slipped and sat down in some shallow water near the bank. At that time I was using an old

Preparing to tail out a salmon from the Lower Pot, River Brora.

11 foot 6 inch double-handed greenheart grilse rod which was not really man enough for the river, and I was having a lot of trouble punching the line out across the wind. Stefa suggested that while she lay in the heather to dry herself (for despite the wind it was sunny) I should borrow her 12 foot 6 inch Farlow cane rod for a spell, and we decided that if there was no

improvement during the next half-hour, we would pack up and go home. The more powerful rod allowed me to cover the water much more efficiently, and I was indulging in casting practice as much as anything when I felt a tug on the line and, lifting my rod tip, found myself into a fish. What a change in our spirits! The water no longer looked dour and dead, the wind was a challenge rather than a nuisance, Stefa's wet trousers were forgotten, and there was no more thought of packing up. In fact that first fish escaped as Stefa tried, perhaps a trifle too enthusiastically, to net it, but she insisted that I carry on with her rod, and in a very short space of time I had hooked another fish, which was landed. After that I resumed my own rod, but we decided to move upstream to a pool called the Upper Fannich where there was a great deal more protection from the wind, which had anyway now abated to some extent. The pool is a long one, running between parallel banks, and the fishing, even in low water, is all from the bank. On this day the water was running strong and high after a spate. I was fishing a 1½-inch articulated black and yellow treble, Stefa a Garry Dog. On it she had the first take, lost contact after a few minutes, cast again and hooked what we were both sure was the same fish. We never saw it, for it threw the hook a second time, but its imperious movement through the water indicated a powerful and heavy fish. From then on it was all frantic action: casting, hooking fish, losing fish and landing fish for each other. There was hardly a moment – or so it seemed in retrospect – when some drama was not in progress. We ended up with three fish apiece, the largest a 10½-pounder caught by Stefa, and never was a heavy load so willingly borne as when we set off for the Ford pool where Tim had arranged to pick us up. Two other anglers, not of our party, had been fishing the Ford and Rallan Pools all afternoon and had had no sport whatever – such are the unpredictable ways of salmon.

Those were autumn fish, of course, some of them very black, and one can only imagine what it would be like to have a similar experience with fresh-run springers. In his little booklet on the lower River Brora, Mr Rob Wilson, doyen of the Brora fishing, tells of fishing the same pool and having four fish on the bank, all over 18 pounds, besides losing four more!

The blackness of the Brora fish struck me, for I was more accustomed to seeing autumn fish that were a rusty red in colour, but the reason for it was revealed one Sunday when we went up the River Blackwater to the remote Ben Armine lodge for a picnic. Here the river was no more than a stony burn a few yards wide, and the salmon that we saw in it were presumably on, or close to, their spawning redds. Often, as a fish moved upstream, its back and dorsal fin would be exposed as it splashed and floundered through a stretch of shallows. To see such large creatures, that not long since had enjoyed the freedom of the ocean, inhabiting such a restricted environment, was one of the strangest natural sights that I have witnessed. As we stood by the burn I saw a fish dart through the water and come to rest in midstream just opposite where we were standing, and I called the attention of my companions to it. But when we looked neither I nor any of the others could see the fish, though we leant over the water and peered at the spot from a distance of no more than a couple of yards. In the end I had to concede the possibility that it had moved further on during the brief moment when I had looked away, but when I took a step into the water, there was a puff of sand and what had seemed to be a boulder among the other black and ochreous boulders on the bed of the stream, shot through the water like a dark missile and vanished upstream. The black colour of these salmon, I realized, was a perfect camouflage for this particular water, where all the stones were shagged with a black algal growth, and good camouflage must be vital to their survival. Presumably, since the majority of salmon are said to return to their native rivers to breed, their autumn coloration is decided genetically, to suit those particular spawning grounds. Undoubtedly a red Devon salmon would show up like a sore thumb in the upper reaches of the Blackwater (whose name may also be significant in this regard) and it would be easy prey to any predator. Potential predators, man apart, might be fewer today, but the otter is one obvious candidate, and in relatively recent times both the osprey and the sea eagle were common throughout the Highlands.

That unforgettable afternoon on the Upper Fannich must have been the last occasion on which I caught a salmon using my old greenheart rod. It reminds me that a fellow guest on one of my visits to the Brora also had a greenheart. Roger was more of a stalker than a fisherman, but one day he decided to spend a day on the river, and produced the mighty weapon with which his grandfather had done battle with great salmon in days of yore. Eighteen foot long, it was complete with brass reel and a line of braided silk. It had a somewhat soft action but otherwise seemed sound enough, and suggestions that a new line might be a good idea were brushed aside: 'What was good enough for my grandfather is good enough for me.' A nylon cast in place of the brittle and yellowed gut with which it was equipped, was his only concession to modernity. The foxed leaves of an old book of flies contained an array of splendidly dressed traditional patterns, and with one of these at the end of his cast, a Durham Ranger maybe or a Mar Lodge, he set to work at the Bengie and very soon, *mirabile dictu*, had hooked a salmon. The great rod flexed its ancient muscles and bent like a willow sapling in a gale, but alas, it was for the last time; with a crack the top section of the rod broke. However, the salmon was still on, and though it was a large fish, and lively, there was still hope of bringing it to the net. Five minutes passed and then, as the fish surged down the pool in a bid for freedom, there was another crack and the mid-section of the rod split in twain. But still the fish was there, and even with the rod reduced to half its length and the line cluttered with the two broken sections, hope was not yet

The merlin is the typical raptor of the heather moorland.

119

dead. 'There is no problem,' said Roger, in tones of lordly confidence, as if this was the manner in which he always caught his fish. 'The fish is exhausted and I will haul him in by hand.' This he proceeded to do, and helpers stood by with the net at the ready. It almost worked, but when the tired fish saw the net it gave a flick of its tail and this was too much for the old silk line. It parted, and though Roger made a desperate lunge for the retreating end, it disappeared from view. Collecting what remained of the ancient rod, he drove into Brora and purchased a new one.

There are so many other scenes that linger in the memory from those autumn days on the Brora: fishing for sea-trout from a boat on Loch Brora under the couchant, leonine shape of the Carol rock, for instance, and the loud, honking calls of a skein of greylags as they flew up and down the shore of the loch. I remember, too, going for a walk one evening up Strath Brora and, in a meadow that sloped to the tree-lined river, coming upon a lonely, fenced-in graveyard and reading the names on the crowded, lichened tombstones, wondering at the isolation of the place, so far from any habitation, and about the harsh lives of those long-dead clansmen. It was a sombre, rather eerie spot, and I was not sorry to move on. Another walk took me into the hills behind the lodge, following the deep ravine through which the Blackwater comes foaming down towards its union with the Brora. Here I watched a little jack merlin as it preened itself, perched on a white boulder in the midst of a great expanse of heather and blaeberry, and later spent a long time watching, through binoculars, the nervous wheeling and huddling of a group of red deer hinds on a mountainside perhaps ¼ mile distant, as rival stags manœuvred around them in their efforts to gain possession of the herd. The stags were black from rolling in peat-haggs, and the clash of antlers, together with their angry grunts and bellows, echoed among the mountains, for the rut was in full swing. Towards evening the deer would forsake the high tops and come down to enjoy the richer grazings of the woods and valleys. Often, returning from the river at dusk, we would come upon a herd feeding on the lush grass at the margin of the loch. They would look up, their eyes fluorescent in the car headlights, but showed little of the wariness or timidity that characterized them in daylight on the tops. At night I would go to sleep to the combined sounds of the falls below the house and the roaring of stags from the woods above. No better lullaby could be imagined.

Ponds and Estuaries

At opposite ends of the game-fishing spectrum are two locales, ponds and estuaries, each of which has its special and quite different attractions.

Ponds might be said to share some of the defects which make me less than enthusiastic about most reservoir fishing: the trout in them, for one thing, are bound to be introduced fish. But they do tend to be secluded and private places, so that at least one does not suffer from the element of being surrounded by too many other human beings, to escape from whom is for me an essential part of the joy of fishing. They have in common with the more mature reservoirs the fact that they are excellent places for observing birds and other forms of wildlife, and their surroundings are generally peaceful and aesthetically pleasing. I think that the actual capture of trout, in such places, is seldom quite as satisfying as the capture of wild fish in rivers or natural lakes, and indeed I have, on occasion, had more excitement and pleasure fishing lowland ponds for carp and tench, or in the winter for pike and large perch, than for stocked trout who do bear, to some extent, the character of interlopers. Coarse fish belong naturally in ponds; they will arrive there without any aid from man and will immediately start to multiply, and I must admit to a bias in favour of what is ecologically appropriate.

Having said that, it would be churlish to deny that I have spent some very happy hours fishing for trout on various ponds, lakes and meres – the terminology seems to be fairly interchangeable – particularly on those where beautiful surroundings were a contributory factor. And there have been excitements too.

In June 1988 I was invited to fish a small lake on a private estate in Suffolk. I went there with Alastair, on a warm and sunny evening, with only a slight breeze to ruffle the surface of the water, and it was an idyllic scene. The lake was L-shaped, covering several acres, and surrounded by parkland. Its waters, deep, clear and dark green, reflected the huge old oaks and horse chestnuts, Scots pines, beeches and willows on its banks and the massed pink flowers of rhododendron bushes that jutted out over the water and flowered right to the water's edge, so that it was hard to tell where the bush ended and the reflections started. There were coots and moorhens, wild duck and dabchicks, and all around the margins of the lake were colonies of toad tadpoles – an abundance of them such as I have not seen for many years. My host told me that in early spring the water had been seething with mating toads.

The lake had been stocked with trout quite a number of years ago, but since then a new lake had been dug which had become the main trout fishery and the old lake, together with the remaining trout, had been left largely to its own devices. We were told that a few trout might still be there, but that several fish had been caught, each of which was presumed, at the time, to be the last survivor. It didn't matter; to drift in the boat or wander the banks on such a lovely evening, with the cries of the waterfowl, and a chorus of birdsong coming from the leaf-heavy trees, and to cast one's fly into the dark, mysterious waters on the chance of some Methuselah of a trout being there to notice it, was pleasure enough.

At about eight o'clock in the evening, Alastair was fishing

from the stern of the boat, anchored some 20 yards out from the bank, with Sam, his large black Labrador dog, sitting demurely in the bows. We had seen no fish rise – though diving dabchick had occasionally startled us with their splashes – and he was casting by this time rather automatically, round the clock, since trout, if any were present, could be anywhere in the lake. He was fishing a no. 6 Alexandra, using a fairly fast retrieve, and the regular 'swish, swish' of his casts became an integral part of the murmurous summer evening sounds. It was an ineffably tranquil scene, as the shadows lengthened across the parkland and the sky reflections on the water turned from blue to shades of bronze and madder. The bird song was augmented now by the cooing of wood pigeons, as with bulging crops and a clatter of wings, they flew into the tops of the tall trees at the far end of the lake. Gnats danced and glinted in the pale sunlight and sedge flies fluttered up from the water, and found refuge among the polished leaves of the rhododendrons.

And then the frankly unexpected happened, and the calm of the evening was shattered. One moment Alastair was fishing with the languid motions of one who, after several hours, had ceased to expect any dramatic change in his fortunes, the next he was in a frenzy of action. With one hand he held his bowed rod aloft as the reel screamed and the line vee'd through the water, while with his other hand he hauled up the mud-weight and secured its rope around the cleat. That he was in to a very good fish was apparent. It ran almost to the end of the lake before turning, taking out most of his backing, and then it came charging back while he reeled in furiously, passed the boat, and took out line again as it made for the other end of the lake. It ran several more times and splashed vigorously on the surface before settling down to a dogged perambulation around the boat. Finally it demonstrated its strength by towing the boat, against the breeze, in towards the bank, and it was here, after a fight that lasted in total just over fifteen minutes, and hampered by the trailing branches

of a weeping willow, that Alastair at last brought it over the net and heaved it up into the dinghy.

It was a lovely fish, perfectly shaped and weighing just 4 pounds. Whether, indeed, it was the last of its kind in the lake is open to speculation, but rumours persist that an even bigger fish has been seen, perhaps 6 pounds, and that it still lurks in those crepuscular green depths, feeding on the crayfish with which the lake is also stocked.

A far cry from the ponds and lakes of lowland Britain are the river estuaries, for these are among the wildest locations in which the game fisherman can pursue his sport. Here the quarry is nearly always the sea-trout. A rod-caught salmon from salt water is a rare occurrence, though why this should be, I cannot imagine. The salmon in fresh water, where it does not feed, will take lures which presumably remind it of the prey on which it had been feeding in the sea, yet in salt water, while still feeding, it will ignore them: just another of the enigmas which make this fish so fascinating. Sea-trout, on the other hand, will readily take representations of sand eels or fry while in salt water. They come up on the flood tide and if no spate or freshet tempts them to continue upriver, they will feed for a few hours among the bladderwrack or over beds of eelgrass before dropping back with the ebb. Some local knowledge is useful in locating the feeding grounds of the shoals, for river estuaries are often extensive and where there is nothing but bare mud the sea-trout are unlikely to linger. I have, myself, only once caught a decent sea-trout from salt water, but it is something of which I would like to do more, for estuaries hold great attractions for the naturalist as well as for the fisherman.

One year I was fishing in the north of Sutherland. On the Sunday, when we could not fish the river, we took a couple of boats out on the Kyle of Tongue. Some amusement was caused by the fact that I was using my old greenheart grilse

Alastair playing a large brown trout on a Suffolk lake.

rod, while everybody else had taken spinning rods – a bigoted purist, evidently! But with a wide selection of spoons and Devon Minnows to choose from, the only obliging fish came to my Teal Blue and Silver. Unfortunately it turned out to be, not a sea-trout, but a whiting! Later that afternoon I walked up to the head of the kyle where a stream flows in from Loch an Dithreibh, and met a young man who had caught two sea-trout, which he showed me. Still using my fly rod, I fished all afternoon from the bank and from an old jetty, on the flood tide and the ebb, but still succeeded in catching no sea trout, although I ended the day with a good basket of saithe.

On another occasion I fished the estuary of the River Dervaig on Mull, and there at least I had the pleasure of seeing many sea-trout very actively feeding among the kelp, swirling on the surface and chasing each other through the water; but although I fished hard for several hours, I could not interest them in any of my lures.

The charm of estuaries was borne in upon me long ago, during my shooting days, when wildfowling was, for me, the quintessence of sport. The fisherman sees them in their less austere summer aspect, but at all times of the year they have the mystery, the wildness and the spice of danger that they owe to being for one half of every twenty-four hours land, and for the other half sea. They teem with life of every kind: strange, amphibious marine creatures, crustaceans, fish, otters and seals, and above all birds. The gulls, the ducks and geese, the herons and all the great tribe of wading birds fill the air with their haunting, wild calls, particularly when the tide is making. And at the flood, when there is only a bland expanse of water and the tortuous windings of the river channel and its tributary creeks are hidden from view, we can gaze at them and imagine, with a quickening of the pulse, the salmon and sea-trout passing like fleet shadows over the

Curlew, Loch Moidart. Sea-trout also feed among the bladderwrack while the tide is in.

sand, impelled by an unaccustomed surge of fresh water and a driving instinct to enter the river and seek, despite all obstacles, the spawning grounds they left as alevins several years before.

Index

Left. *The estuary of the Iorsa Water, Isle of Arran.*